Democracy and Discontent

PROGRESSIVISM,
SOCIALISM AND SOCIAL CREDIT
IN THE CANADIAN WEST

Walter D. Young

RYERSON PRESS
McGRAW-HILL COMPANY OF CANADA LIMITED

TORONTO · MONTREAL · NEW YORK · LONDON · SYDNEY
JOHANNESBURG · MEXICO · PANAMA · DÜSSELDORF · SINGAPORE
RIO DE JANEIRO · KUALA LUMPUR · NEW DELHI

SBN 7700 0271 4

Acknowledgments
Where necessary, permission to quote
copyrighted material has been sought
through the publishers noted in the
relevant places.

The illustrations in this book have
been obtained from the following sources:
Manitoba Archives, p. 20
Public Archives of Canada, pp. 30, 31, 48, 50, 90
The Toronto Star Syndicate, p. 42
Karsh, Ottawa, p. 64
The Winnipeg Free Press, pp. 73, 94
Canadian Press, p. 97

The publisher wishes to acknowledge with
gratitude those who have given their
permission to use copyrighted material in
this book. Every effort has been made to
credit all sources correctly. The author and
publisher will welcome information that will
allow them to correct any errors or omissions.

Charts by D. Hayward

2 3 4 5 6 7 8 9 RC-69 8 7 6 5 4 3 2 1
PRINTED AND BOUND IN CANADA

Foreword

From an early date, conditions in western Canada prompted political protest. This new frontier had appeared so promising that settlers were particularly resentful when serious problems arose. Farmer and worker began to suspect that the existing political parties, with their roots in the east, were not responding to very real economic hardships in the west. Consequently, westerners looked for alternative solutions.

The story of this search is recounted in *Democracy and Discontent*, the second volume to be published in *The Frontenac Library*. To bring a sense of immediacy to past events, Dr. Young has quoted from important original sources. To show how opinions differ, he has assessed the interpretations of other scholars, not in order to refute them, but to assess their place in a continuing debate. It is worth noting that protest movements in the west have attracted the attention of scholars in sister disciplines, especially sociologists and political scientists. Dr. Young's volume, therefore, like those of other authors in *The Library*, provides the reader with issues for personal assessment and analysis.

Democracy and Discontent illuminates a permanent Canadian dilemma. Given the regionalism and economic diversity of the country, the working of a just, democratic system is far from easy; the story of the Progressives, the Social Credit Party and the CCF may help us to understand how it is possible.

G.M.

Preface

The purpose of this book is to bring together and summarize some of the material concerning the development of protest movements and parties in the Canadian west. As such it is intended to serve as a convenient introduction to the study of radical politics in Canada.

There is particular merit in focusing attention on the period that saw the rise of social credit and socialism, side-by-side, from the same landscape. Because they are unique in Canadian experience and stand slightly off the most highly travelled roads of Canadian history, the study of these movements and parties offers insights into the operation of the Canadian party system, into the inter-relationship of economic, geographic and social factors, and into the nature of democracy itself. And, obviously, the events of those desperate years between the two wars reach forward to affect the events of today.

It is a rather seedy truism that the past shapes and influences the present. It requires no feat of intellectual agility to see that what happened in Alberta, Saskatchewan and Manitoba in the thirties changed the shape of Canadian politics. It is important to note, however, that most histories of Canada treat the development of the CCF and Social Credit parties lightly—as though they were examples of western madness: the Calgary Stampede in politics. If it succeeds in its aims this book should help to create a more balanced perspective.

Another good reason for studying the growth of social protest in the Canadian west is that a fair amount of material has already been written on it. Social Credit has been studied more thoroughly than any other political phenomenon in Canada—with the possible exception of the British North America Act.

To a lesser degree the same is true of the CCF. This fact points to the significance of these party-movements—or, perhaps, to the fondness of historians and social scientists for studying exotica.

Several dimensions of the history of protest are covered in the pages that follow. The focus, in the case of Social Credit, is largely provincial for it was at this level that the movement had its greatest impact. The Progressives, on the other hand, were organized for an assault on Ottawa and only in Manitoba did they make any headway in provincial politics—unless one views the United Farmers of Alberta as a branch, in which case they did rather well in that province as well. The CCF is also treated largely as a national movement, although, clearly, it was a success in Saskatchewan. The limitations of space and the availability of material seemed to make this a reasonable approach.

The manuscript for this book was written during part of a sabbatical leave that was assisted by a Canada Council grant. I am grateful to Mrs. Joan Dow who did the typing, and particularly to my wife Beryl for reading and criticizing the drafts and helping with the proofreading and index, always with patience and persistence.

Finally, I would like to dedicate the book to Jeremy, Margot, and Brian whose enthusiasm and interest in the project added greatly to the pleasure of writing it.

W.D.Y.
Saltspring Island

Contents

Acknowledgments   iv

Foreword   v

Preface   vi

INTRODUCTION: *The Fires of Progress*   ix

CHAPTER I
The Roots of Discontent   1

CHAPTER II
The Manifestation of Discontent   14

CHAPTER III
The Progressives   29

CHAPTER IV
The Great Depression   40

CHAPTER V
The CCF, 1932-1945   57

CHAPTER VI
The CCF: Left, Right and Centre   69

CHAPTER VII
The Coming of Social Credit   80

CHAPTER VIII
Practice and the Preacher   92

CHAPTER IX
Parliament and Protest   105

Time Chart   112

Notes   114

Bibliographical Note   117

Index   120

Introduction: The Fires of Progress

In a democratic society we grow accustomed to the established machinery through which people may, if they choose, express their points of view and work to bring about the changes they desire. This machinery functions on the assumption that the views people hold are consistent with the continued existence of the system, although there may be some desire for minor changes. In other words, democracy is a form of government that does not assume the need for fundamental or revolutionary change.

In actual practice, people seldom make use of the machinery of public expression. Many people write letters to their Member of Parliament complaining about some minor injustice, or letters to the newspaper protesting some government act or some policy of the city council. But overall, people who have legitimate grievances constitute a minority, and a disparate minority at that. For example, not all the letter writers have pension problems; not all dislike the new zoning regulations; nor do all of them oppose the fluoridation of the water supply. There is nothing to bring them together to make common cause for the purpose of bringing about the changes they seek. They do not all seek the same changes or see the same wrongs. When dissent is random in this fashion it is fair to say that the political system is working reasonably well. It would be foolish to expect any system to please all the people all the time.

As long as the few with a complaint can get a hearing, and as long as the many can change governments periodically through the electoral process, then we have a stable and working democracy. But it occasionally happens that a lot of people share a grievance or several grievances, and that the government, for a variety of reasons, is insensitive to their demands. Or it may be that the existing form of government is not built to include their demands.

Faced with such insensitivity, the individuals concerned often come together, focusing their demands, sharpening their case and presenting a united front. The emergence of a single individual with a dominant personality may bring about a coalition of the discontented, or the acceptance of a single explanation of their plight. A specific body of proposals for remedy may cause the dissident minority to band together to press their claims. In doing so, they not only make their voices louder, they also increase their own awareness of their position, sharing, so to speak, the discomforts of their neighbour. This, in turn, strengthens their determination and adds further to their unity.

MOVEMENTS AND PARTIES

When a large number of people come together in order to bring about fundamental changes in their society or in some major institution of that society, they are referred to, collectively, as a movement. A distinction can be made between social and political movements in terms of their objectives and the methods they use. But, since most "social" movements impinge upon the political sector, and since "political" movements invariably impinge upon the social sector, there seems to be little point in making the distinction here.

There is a clear difference between a movement and a political party, however, and it is useful to keep it in mind. In general, political parties are organizations whose purpose is the election of a sufficient number of their members to win and hold control of the government. They usually seek to do this within the framework of a body of doctrine referred to as their philosophy or, more loosely, as their ideology. This body of doctrine may or may not be evident in the party platform at election time. In practice most major parties strive to look like the other major parties without, at the same time, destroying the appearance of difference.

Political parties are not, as a rule, noted for their anxiety to bring about sweeping social and political change; movements are. Herein lies the chief difference between a party and a movement. Parties would rather win elections than converts—

unless, of course, winning converts would win them the election. Some movements enter the political arena in order to achieve their goals. They adopt the methods and mantle of the political parties, although they are never quite comfortable with them. It often occurs that a movement grows more like a party until, in fact, it becomes one. Then winning office is the prime goal; bringing about change is secondary.

In the case of the movements discussed in this book, all were actively involved in politics. All began on the great plains of the Canadian west and were shaped by the problems of the wheat farmer. One, the Co-operative Commonwealth Federation (CCF), included significant non-farm elements. It became and remained a major influence in national politics. Another, the Social Credit movement, remained essentially rural in support and outlook and was never of any real significance in national politics. The third, the Progressive movement, burst upon the political scene in 1920, only to evaporate in less than ten years, largely because of its inability to cope with the strain of transition from the status of a movement to that of a party.

The appearance of the Progressive movement, with the CCF and Social Credit in its train, did not only mean that the farmers and the radicals in the west and in some of the eastern cities were determined to enter politics to better their lot; it meant also that the two-party system in Canada had disappeared. Parliament was no longer to be a forum for two groups—government and opposition, the "ins" and the "outs". It was to become more representative of the different shades of opinion across Canada. While the party in power was always either Liberal or Conservative, that party had, of necessity, to pay more attention to the demands of those citizens who were represented in Ottawa first by the Progressives and later by the CCF and Social Credit.

As the new movements flexed their muscles and found in politics a way of moving closer to their goals, the dominance of the two old parties in provincial politics also came to an end. In 1919 the United Farmers of Ontario swept into power in a provincial election. They were swept out again in 1923, but the die had been cast. In 1921 in Alberta, the Farmers' party, later the United Farmers of Alberta, won thirty-eight out of fifty-eight seats to bring about the end of the dominance of the "old line" parties in that province. A year later the United Farmers of

Manitoba formed a government in their province. Saskatchewan elected a CCF government in 1944 and British Columbia elected a Social Credit administration in 1952.

The appearance of the west as somehow unique in Canadian politics was not actually a sudden reversal of form. It was not as if these provinces had been like all the others before 1920 and had then suddenly become radical. The west was the frontier and it was growing in a way the other provinces were not. It was, one might say, on the edge of Canada, and needed either constant reassurance of its attachment to the rest of the country or a solid sense of its own identity. Because the former was lacking, demonstrably so in the immediate postwar period, the west opted for the latter. The distance between the western provinces and the centres of power and decision in Canada was very real in the physical sense—for example, Ottawa is 1,700 miles from Regina. It was also very real in political and economic terms. To achieve power and influence, if only to force the government of the day to pay attention to them, the western farmers went into politics. By membership in the movements and parties which they had created and which they controlled, they established an identity for themselves that they did not have in the eastern dominated Liberal and Conservative parties.

INTERPRETING THE PAST

Historians and social scientists who have studied the social and political ferment that typified the Canadian west between the wars have generally not disagreed violently in their interpretations. The isolation of the west, the nature of the economy and the physical setting have all been cited as significant. The differences in interpretation have tended to be in emphasis. For example, S. M. Lipset, a sociologist, has argued that the nature of Canadian political institutions—the federal parliamentary system—was the most significant factor in the development of "one-party politics" in Alberta. By comparison, C. B. Macpherson, a political scientist, has said that a more important factor was the economic structure of the province which produced a class consciousness that gave impetus to the Social Credit movement. John Irving has placed greater emphasis on the psychological factors, including the power of William Aberhart's personality and the effective use he made of radio. As stated here, these views are over-simplified, but they indicate the approaches taken by scholars.

It is difficult to resist the temptation to provide an analysis within the framework of a single theory, particularly since the process of historiography—the writing of history—must consist of explanation as well as elucidation. It is for this reason that *the* history of any event will never be written. With each passing year, as different scholars study an event using different techniques and different frameworks for their analyses, new dimensions are added to the original picture. For example, contemporaneous observers of the Winnipeg general strike in 1919, with the story of the Russian Revolution fresh in their minds, and raised to discredit and suspect those elements that attempted to interfere with the free operation of the capitalist system, saw that strike as the first stage of a plan to "sovietize" Canada. With the perspective of passing years and the presentation of carefully gathered evidence, subsequent interpretations of the event have differed markedly from that held by many Canadians in 1919.

It is on carefully gathered evidence that the historian must rest his case. It is not enough to say that the CCF was the inheritor of the Progressive tradition; the assertion must be proven through the presentation of evidence. Evidence used by historians and social scientists is gathered from an ever widening array of sources. At one time the presentation of facts from documents and contemporary reports was sufficient; today the search for evidence includes, where possible, careful analysis of interviews with people involved, scrutiny of voting records, newspapers, financial statements, living conditions, climate and geography. In fact, anything that may have had a bearing on the event and can be subjected to impartial examination is considered. To be an historian then, one must also be something of an economist, sociologist, psychologist, political scientist and geographer. History, as the relationship between man and his environment through time, is never complete. Each historian sees an event or series of events from the perspective of his own time and his own place. Subsequent historians will deal with him as he dealt with the events in his work.

*　　*　　*

In the pages that follow, the birth and growth of some of the protest movements and parties that rose in the Canadian west will be examined; and some of the more significant factors that led to their development will be discussed. In a book of this size selection of events and evidence is obviously crucial—more has been left out than has been included. The aim is simply to provide an introduction to some aspects of this period in Canadian history and to generate an interest in events that still exert marked influence on Canadian politics and society.

To begin, something must be said about the conditions of the period between the wars when frustration, bred of dashed hopes and economic depression, brought about the groundswell of protest that broke on the citadel of power in the east and began to erode the political dominance of central Canada.

Chapter I

The Roots of Discontent

Protest movements and the political parties that sometimes grow out of them do not spring fully armed from the furrowed brow of discontent. They grow and develop slowly, particularly when they represent—as all significant movements must—a break with conventional behaviour. People do not lightly reject the institutions and norms of behaviour they have been raised and educated to respect. When people do seek to change or destroy previously accepted institutions it is usually because they have reached a position, for whatever reasons, where they can no longer continue to live as before; they have reached a point where their frustration, anger or suffering demand relief, and relief requires change.

No single cause brings people to the point where they seek to change their society, although a single cause may be the catalyst that fires the accumulation of discontent. The Canadian protest movements discussed in this book were the product of many factors. The most significant were geography, economics and politics. These affected not only how people lived, how they earned—or failed to earn—their living, but how they thought and reacted to each other and to the rest of Canada.

THE FARMER AND THE LABOURER IN THE WEST

The 1,000,000 people who came in the early years of the twentieth century from Europe, the United States and Ontario to the great plains of western Canada, to homestead and farm, did not come to a land of milk and honey. The price of wheat in those years was generally higher than it had been for some time and prosperity did seem to most of them to be within reach. But the homesteaders were almost entirely dependent upon this one factor—the price of wheat—and it was quite beyond their control. Indeed, one common denominator among the settlers was that they were not masters of their own fate.

1

This situation was paradoxical, for many of the settlers had elected to homestead in the Canadian west in order to achieve the solid independence and self-reliance of the farmer. The appeal of the agrarian life was its reputed simplicity, honesty, and guaranteed prosperity; after all, people always need food. It was on the frontier, out on the farthest reaches of civilization, that a man could be himself, carving a livelihood for his family from the rich soil of the plain, beholden to none but his Creator and himself. Or so it was thought.

Gradually the prairie farmer came to discover the truth of his situation. The frontier meant isolation more than it meant independence—isolation from his fellows, from the marketing centres and from the centres of political power. He found himself marooned on an island of semi-fertile soil in a sea of grass. In addition the prairie farmer had no control over the elements, yet the elements determined how he lived. If it was too cold or too dry or too wet, his crop brought him a low return and there was nothing he could do about it.

The hardships and isolation imposed by geography and climate in themselves provided a basis for discontent; the economic condition of the prairie farmer exacerbated the situation. He was tied to one crop, wheat. It was a product for which the price was unstable, fluctuating with the supply in the world market and the activities of speculators on the Winnipeg Grain Exchange. The price might be high, as it was at the turn of the century, or it might be low, as it was in 1913 and again in the 1920's. The farmer, however, had no control over the price he received for his crop; all he could do was accept it. Moreover, even at the best of times, the major profits in the grain market went to those who bought and sold on the grain exchange; many of them had never been near a farm. For the farmer, dependence on wheat meant constant instability and insecurity. It is significant that the organs of government that could have legislated to solve some of the wheat farmer's problems, were singularly insensitive to his demands and, in the case of the federal government, out of reach and out of touch.

A typical prairie farmer had purchased his land (or mortgaged his homestead for ready cash) from a land company. The largest of these was the Canada Northwest Land Company, a subsidiary of the Canadian Pacific Railway. In most cases, therefore, the farmer had mortgage payments to meet. In addition, his worldly goods and his farm implements had been purchased from eastern manufacturers who were protected by the high tariff wall of John A. Macdonald's National Policy, a tariff wall that Laurier's Liberal party was unwilling to pull down. Bruce Hutchison wrote of the prairie farmer:

> Here was a man who worked harder than any labourer in the factories of Ontario . . . who had to plow, disc, seed, reap and thresh two or three acres merely to pay for a small mechanical part to repair his tractor, when it could be bought for a fraction of the price on the other side of the American boundary, the tariff wall.

> It would cost $25. If he could get it from the States, without paying the tariff, it would cost maybe $10 or $5. This is the tribute the prairies pay to the eastern manufacturer. . . .[1]

The farmer sowed his wheat and hoped that there would be no late frost or drought or rust, or locusts, or heavy rains, or early frost. When he harvested the grain, he took it to the railhead and there had it graded by an employee of the elevator company— possibly a subsidiary of the CPR—and was paid for it on the basis of the grade and the going price for that grade at that time. Often the price rose subsequent to his delivery, but this increase did not find its way into his pockets; it went to the elevator companies, the speculators and the railroads. Life for the farmer, like the return for his labours, was marginal and insecure. The west was a debtor region, and honest toil brought few rewards.

G. MacEwan wrote:

> . . . this centralization of power at a point somewhat remote from the actual farmer and in the hands of business men who did not always realize his problems produced a feeling of distrust in the agricultural community which soon grew to antagonism. The relation was too close between the financial houses, the grain dealers, the milling companies, and the railroads. Many of the milling companies operated their own elevators. The associated dealers were in a position to fix prices. The railways would not accept loading except through the elevators. There was a monopolistic flavour about the whole thing.[2]

It was clear to the farmer that the real control of his destiny was in the hands of those who owned the land companies and the elevator companies, and those who ran the Grain Exchange. It was also clear to him that these people had more political influence. The parties were controlled by the same financial interests in the east that controlled the companies with whom the farmers had to deal. It made little difference to the farmer which party was in power. To him both were the same—singularly unresponsive to his needs. The real centres of power were in the east and easterners had a vested interest in keeping the western farmer in a condition of feudal dependence.

The result of this situation was inevitable. The farmers soon came to distrust political parties. Accustomed to the straightforward nature of his own existence, he saw politics and politicians as devious and dishonest, and the party system as obsolete and degenerate.

In the cities of the west where there was industry and a working class—Winnipeg, Calgary, Edmonton, Vancouver—there was similar discontent. Urban discontent was not caused by the same factors that brought the wheat farmer to a realization of the injustice of his position, but the city worker in the west also came to see the established political parties and their backers (the economic élite) as his enemies. The economic slump of 1913-1915 brought unemployment. Although the 1914-1918 war gave the economy a needed boost, it brought higher prices but no parallel increase in wages. Yet those who owned businesses and factories often profited handsomely from the war effort. The distinction between the rich and the poor became increasingly obvious. As a result, the labourers in the cities began to develop a class consciousness.

The harsh inequality that was so easily observed in the big cities was a clear denial of the ideals of democracy as the working class understood them. The advantages of the free enterprise system were reserved for a few. The ideal of a competitive economy meant "survival of the fittest" in an unfair contest. The anomalies of Canadian society in the west were no greater than in the east; in the west, however, they were more clearly defined and therefore more obvious.

There were some differences between east and west, however, which help to explain the success of radical movements in the west and their absence in the east. The west was isolated from the centres of economic and political power. On the frontier the prairie farmer was virtually in a feudal relationship to the magnates of the east. In addition, the nature of the population in the west ensured that a body of economic and political thought was planted that bore the fruit of political revolt.

The population of the west during the boom years of 1896-1911 came primarily from three sources: Ontario, the United states and Europe—primarily Great Britain. Those from Ontario settled largely in Manitoba; Saskatchewan received a higher proportion of British; Alberta attracted a higher proportion of Americans than the other two. Settlers coming from Britain and the United States possessed knowledge and experience of radical political movements in their homelands. Many of the British immigrants were familiar with the ideas of the Labour party, and many of the American settlers had belonged to one or other of the farmers' movements in the United States, such as the Grange or Patrons of Industry. Some had been involved in the more political movements, such as the Non-Partisan League and the American Progressive party. Among those from Britain and the United States there was a readiness to seek out and find the source of the trouble and to focus the discontent, giving it direction and purpose. The settlers who moved west from Ontario were, by contrast, less radical, and more eager to accept the existing system given some basic economic reform.

In British Columbia the division between the classes was harsh and clear. In that province the power of the timber barons and the mining companies was obvious and their influence on the provincial government unquestionable. There was no agrarian population to speak of and relatively little manufacturing. The economy was based on primary production: logging, mining and fishing. In the case of the first two industries, large numbers of men were employed outside the cities and, necessarily, housed and fed by the companies. They were thoroughly dominated by their employers. The conditions of the work meant continual risk and discomfort.

The nature of the mining and logging economies was not unlike that of the wheat economy: primary production, largely for export and consequently sensitive to fluctuations in the world market. Employers simply shut down operations when the prices for timber and minerals were too low to be economic. The result was insecurity for the miners and loggers. Here again lay fertile soil for the radical ideas brought by immigrants from Britain and the United States. It is not surprising that, lacking the moderating effect proprietorship (ownership of land and equipment) had upon the wheat farmer, protest politics in Canada's most western province were more radical than anywhere else.

At the turn of the century trade unionism in British Columbia was advancing, led by the radical Western Federation of Miners. In the wake of employer opposition to unions there were strikes in the mines, on the fishing grounds and in the factories. Corruption in government, poor conditions in the mines and the influx of Chinese labour aggravated the situation and fed the flames being fanned by organizers from radical American unions. The Vancouver *News Advertiser* wrote in 1901:

> An active socialist propaganda is proceeding at Nelson, and in the Slocan riding—the latter more especially and as large numbers of the miners are naturalized Americans of Populist views, they scarcely need conversion to socialism. Meanwhile the socialism that is amongst us naturally feeds and grows upon the fact that in the quite recent past wholly inordinate concessions of public rights and property have been made almost unrestrictedly ... to companies, combines and individuals who have frequently failed to give anything like adequate value to the community in return.[3]

The open exploitation of the province's wealth for private benefit with the clear connivance of the government encouraged the growing socialist movement and simplified the process of gaining converts.

Despite the apparent similarity of their condition, the western farmer and worker did not make common cause until the formation of the Co-operative Commonwealth Federation in 1932. There was, indeed, some antagonism between the two groups. The farmer was frequently an employer of labour and, understandably, unsympathetic toward the worker's demands for an eight-hour day. The farmer's attitudes were those of the small proprietor and he liked to think he was his own boss.

Yet the similarities between farmers and workers are more striking than the differences during the period under discussion.

Both groups found their world hostile, they seemed to be aliens in their own land, not achieving the fulfillment of the promises they had seen when they first emigrated. The political system and the economic system had turned sour on them.

THE EXPRESSION OF DISCONTENT

The feelings of discontent among western farmers and working men were given apt expression by some clergymen who saw in the state of society a contradiction of the Christian gospels. Men like Salem Bland, William Irvine and J. S. Woodsworth preached the social gospel from their pulpits, stressing the importance of love, the superiority of co-operation to competition, and the application of the Sermon on the Mount to everyday life. It was a creed that was concerned with the welfare and behaviour of the individual in *this* world. The question of salvation was of minor importance; what mattered was the human condition. These men were outraged by a society that set wealth as a goal, and in which the achievement of wealth was used to justify a wide range of behaviour. They saw in the slums of Winnipeg the wretched products of this system.

From his pulpit Woodsworth attacked the "Sin of Indifference":

> A curse still hangs over inactivity. A severe condemnation still rests upon indifference . . . . Christianity stands for social righteousness as well as personal righteousness . . . . It is quite right for me to be anxious to save my never dying soul; but it is of greater importance to try to serve the present age. . . .

> There have been socialists and positivists and secularists and agnostics who, by their sincerity and earnestness and self-sacrificing spirit, have put to shame many of the professed followers of Christ . . . . If it is right to help the sick, it is right to do away with filth and overcrowding, and to provide sunlight and good air and good food. We have tried to provide *for the poor*. Yet, have we tried to alter the social conditions that lead to poverty?

> You can't separate a man from his surroundings and deal separately with each.[4]

This was the social gospel that led these men inevitably away from their pulpits into the streets and, eventually, into the arena of politics.

This response was not typical of churchmen. The church generally represented the establishment, the social élite in the community, and seldom challenged the prevailing values. In contrast, Woodsworth and those like him attacked the élite and their values. They entered the arena on the side of the poor, and in the case of Woodsworth and Irvine, entered politics to champion their cause and their beliefs. The social gospel was a gospel of good works, of social service and co-operation, and its preachers were its most active practitioners. For this they earned the rebuke of their churches and were either forced to leave the church or, as Woodsworth did, found membership so intolerable that they resigned.

Farmers and workers responded to the social gospel, for it made sense to them at a time when it seemed nothing else did. With the strength of the Gospels it reinforced views expressed by agrarian and labour leaders. It offered a solution to pressing problems that was consistent with moral values. Disturbed by the failure of their honest toil to reap its just reward, the farmer and the worker sought an answer that was both readily applicable to their situation and easily understood. The social gospel offered an explanation consistent with both religious belief and much that the political radicals were saying.

The doctrines of co-operation and fundamental equality were part of the socialist philosophy expressed by many farm and labour leaders. The two combined to provide a trenchant and incontrovertible analysis of the reasons for the social ills in the west. They offered a course of action and a target. Basically, both demonstrated that the misfortunes of the working class were not of their own making; they were the result of the greed and insensitivity of the wealthy. The correction of this injustice lay within the grasp of the farmers and workers themselves. They had to unite with those like themselves and wrestle with the elements in society as the farmer wrestled with the physical elements.

ORGANIZATION OF THE DISCONTENTED

Before the turn of the century farmers had begun to organize. The economic boom preceding the war of 1914-1918 slowed but did not halt the growth of agrarian groups. The impetus for the development of these movements came from the United States where farmers had banded together to protect their mutual interests. The vulnerability of the single farmer was overcome by united action. By 1905 there were grain growers' associations in Alberta, Saskatchewan and Manitoba. The main purpose of these organizations was to educate their members in collective action, to inform them of their legal and political rights, and the significance and dignity of their calling. The grain growers' associations united the farmers and convinced them of their importance in society.

In 1905 the first farmer-owned grain marketing company was established in Canada. The effectiveness of this organization was soon demonstrated when the Manitoba government forced the Winnipeg Grain Exchange to grant the farmers' company a seat on the exchange. The provincial governments in the west were soon conscious of the growing strength of such farmers' bodies and sought to appease them.

By 1910 the grain growers' associations were strong. They had their own newspaper, *The Grain Growers' Guide*. Through the pages of the *Guide* the farmers developed a consciousness of their strength and unity of purpose. From the *Guide* it is clear that the farmers' attitudes were essentially based on a faith in democracy, a hatred of corporate wealth and a distrust of the prevailing political system.

The Grain Growers' Guide was usually one step ahead of the associations for which it spoke. For example, when the associations were begining to think about political activity, the *Guide* was insisting on it. The *Guide* analysed the problem in this way:

> The root of the evil lies largely in our economic system. It corrupts our political system, our political system corrupts and degrades the public administration, and the corroding influence extends to the social system and business life till the disease pervades the whole community. [5]

The solution was equally simple; a populist democracy should be instituted—that is, one in which the citizens not only control the legislator but actively engage in the legislative process themselves. This goal could be achieved by use of the recall, the initiative and the referendum—techniques advocated by the Populist movement in the United States.

The recall was a means of controlling the elected representative by making him directly responsible to a specified percentage of his electorate through a committee of the electorate. This committee would hold the representative's signed but undated resignation. Should he fail to represent his constituents adequately, the resignation would be dated and submitted to the Speaker of the legislature. The device was applied in a few constituencies in 1921 but never used and was subsequently declared illegal.

The initiative was a process whereby a stated number of people could propose legislation which would then be placed before the whole electorate in the form of a referendum. Because the farmers had lost faith in the existing political institutions and the politicians that manipulated them, they wanted to reform them in such a way that the citizen, as much as possible, became the legislator.

The many socialist and labour parties that were coming into existence at this same time offered similar analyses of the causes of discontent, but the solutions they proposed were more radical and couched in the rhetoric of Marxist socialism. In describing the newly formed Socialist Party, the *Western Clarion* in 1903 said:

> The Socialist Party is not a half way party . . . it aims at peaceful revolution. While the Socialist Party aims ultimately to secure working class ownership of government, to have collective ownership of all the means of producing and distributing wealth, to end the class struggle . . . to abolish wars . . . to give the workers the full product of their toil, the socialist legislators are pledged to introduce and vote for all legislation which aims to improve the material conditions of the working class. [6]

The socialist parties were, for the most part, prepared to support any other group or movement that aimed to improve the existing conditions of the working class. They had much in common with the farmers' movements; they provided the same kind of social nucleus for working men isolated in logging camps, mines, railway work camps in the wilderness, or in urban slum ghettoes. The agrarian reform movements preached the doctrine that the farmers' calling was a noble one, that through collective action the farmer could achieve recognition and his just reward. The social gospel reinforced this view with the scripture. So, too, the doctrines of the socialist and labour parties sought to dignify the toil of the labourer and urged collective action to right wrongs. The activities of both groups provided a social centre for people who felt themselves cut off or alienated. Both emphasized the importance of study and self-improvement. In the case of the Socialist party of British Columbia, much time was spent in the discussion and analysis of the writings of Marx and Engels. Membership in the party was at one point restricted to those who could demonstrate a sound knowledge of Marxist doctrine.

From the turn of the century to the outbreak of World War I there was general prosperity in Canada. Until 1913 the price of wheat was high and settlers streamed into the prairies. There was an investment boom in railway construction and industry elsewhere in Canada. But farmers were increasingly restless as they agitated, without success, for freer trade. The defeat of the government of Sir Wilfrid Laurier on the issue of reciprocity with the United States hardened the resolve of the farmers to press their demands, through independent political action if necessary. The fall in the price of wheat and the resulting hardship between 1913 and 1915 served to remind them that without more active government support their livelihood was precarious. Rising prices during the war and the imposition of manpower registration followed by conscription in 1917 intensified the farmer's sense of grievance.

By the time the war had ended the political situation had ripened considerably for third-party activity. The Liberals, weakened by their defeat in 1911 on the two issues of the naval bill and reciprocity, and finally torn apart by conscription, were in a state of sad disarray in the west. Leading western Liberals such as Sir Clifford Sifton, had sided with Robert Borden's Conservative Unionist government. More than ever the Liberal party seemed to the westerner to be an eastern machine, firmly based in Quebec. The vacuum left in the west by the Liberal decline was to be filled by the Progressive party in 1921.

The sense of grievance felt by the farmers as a result of registration and conscription was shared by the trade union movement. The Trades and Labour Congress had disapproved of both measures, while the rank and file union members, feeling the pinch of high prices and low wages, vehemently criticised those who were making great profits from war contracts. The farm and labour movements alike demanded the conscription of wealth as well as manpower.

The union movement in Canada had been growing steadily, but slowly, since the turn of the century. The Trades and Labour Congress, an organization made up largely of craft unions, was formed in 1886. By 1914 there were 166,000 trade union members in Canada, most of them in unions affiliated with the TLC. Trade unions were not warmly welcomed in Canadian society— nor anywhere else for that matter—because they were seen initially as an unwarranted interference with the free action of the market and as a deliberate affront to the rights of private property. What rights they gained for their members were won inch by inch through strikes—some of them marked by violence and bloodshed. The unions' aims were to assure their members of decent wages and working conditions through the application of collective bargaining, with the strike as their ultimate weapon.

By the end of World War I trade union membership had climbed to 374,000, but this was still much less than half of the total working force and excluded many industrial workers who could not fit into the skilled-craft definition of the unions affiliated with the Trades and Labour Congress. The organization of the semi-skilled and unskilled workers employed in factory, forest and mine, proceeded slowly until the postwar period when the influence of the American industrial unions was more clearly felt. In the west the trade unionists grew restless with the conservatism of the eastern leadership of the Trades and Labour Congress and were frustrated by its refusal to endorse industrial unions. After the war, uneasiness about the future combined with this dissatisfaction; when faced with the refusal of many employers to grant collective bargaining rights and higher wages, the western trade unions grew more militant. Severe labour unrest followed, leading to the Winnipeg general strike and sympathetic strikes in other cities in Canada.

* * *

By the end of World War I, the frustrated expectations of the prairie farmer had become more sharply focused through the influence of the various grain growers' associations and the ideas of men like Henry Wise Wood. The growth of trade unionism and the elaboration of radical political and economic doctrines by western trade union leaders had begun to bring to the urban worker a consciousness of the vulnerability of his position and of the potential offered by organized action. At this same time, the political system in Canada was not able to meet the demands of an increasingly diversified society. The rigidities of party discipline in a parliamentary system denied the flexibility that was necessary and ensured that control of the parties remained in the hands of established interests in eastern Canada. The only viable course of action open to the discontented groups was direct action— confrontation with established authority in an attempt to create a more equitable balance of interests. Paradoxically, labour made the first move in that direction.

Chapter II

The Manifestation of Discontent

The period immediately following the war of 1914-1918 saw the growth of two forces in Canadian politics that had hitherto exerted little influence. Politicians had been aware of the existence of the various farmers' groups, and trade unions had not been unknown; but neither had ever before impinged as directly or forcefully on the nation's political consciousness as they now began to do. For labour this period marked the beginning of a long and slow march toward a place of influence on the political scene. For the farmers it was the culmination of a process that had begun much earlier; it was in the twenties that the farmers' organizations burst upon the scene as a political power. The first of these two forces to come to public attention in the immediate postwar period was labour.

THE EMERGENCE OF ORGANIZED LABOUR

The war had been a period of considerable growth in the trade unions. Membership doubled between 1914 and 1919. However, there had also been signs of a growing division between the eastern and western wings of the trade union movement. More radical than their eastern brothers, the western labour leaders— many of whom were also active in socialist parties—were particularly incensed when the federal government banned the publication of radical literature. Their anger was heightened by the participation of Canadian forces in the counter-revolutionary exercise of the allied powers in Russia in 1918–19. The success of the revolution in Russia had stirred the enthusiasm of radicals in Canada as it had the world over. Many agreed with the contention of Bob Russell when he spoke to a Winnipeg gathering sponsored by the Socialist Party of Canada in 1918: "Capitalism has come to a point where she is defunct and must disappear."[1] All that was needed was a good push.

The radical western trade unionists broke with the more conservative Trades and Labour Congress after the 1918 convention. At that gathering their resolutions calling for the reorganization of the TLC as a congress of industrial unions had been defeated along with one that criticised the government for anti-labour policies and would have banned government appointees from holding office in the Congress.

The western members decided to hold their own convention in Calgary the following year. Their purpose was to organize a new union to be known as the One Big Union, or the OBU. It was to be patterned after the American Industrial Workers of the World (generally known as the "Wobblies"), which was itself a product of western discontent with the conservatism and insularity of the eastern trade union establishment. The OBU, like the IWW, believed that all workers, skilled and unskilled, should join together in a single big union. There were only two classes of people as far as OBU philosophy was concerned, those who were exploited and their exploiters. Like the farmers' movement, though much more radical in tone, the OBU aimed to place the control of industry in the hands of the labour units, thereby destroying the power of the outside interests that had exerted such significant control over the lives of the workers.

The Calgary convention saw close to 200 western trade unionists gather and proclaim their determination to set up locals of the One Big Union in their cities. The debate at the convention and the final declaration, that "the principle of Proletarian Dictatorship . . . [is] absolute and efficient for the transformation of capitalist private property to communal wealth,"[2] demonstrated that the labour leaders were for the most part, dedicated socialists. It was also shown that the delegates had lost all confidence in the established methods of political activity. Isolated from those who controlled the industries they worked, and isolated even from their fellow unionists in the east, geographically and now ideologically, they responded by challenging the system that had produced the situation.

The strength of socialist sentiment among OBU leaders and their openly expressed admiration and respect for the Soviet system of government made the members of the OBU immediately suspect in the eyes of the Canadian government and the leading figures in their respective communities. The language of Marxism was not only foreign to the ears of respectable Winnipeg or Vancouver, it alarmed businessmen across the country. Trade unions at the best of times were considered with suspicion. Those with radical aims, that spoke of the dictatorship of the proletariat and the overthrow of the capitalist system, were downright terrifying. It is not surprising that the Royal North-West Mounted Police (now RCMP) planted undercover agents in the OBU—as indeed they did in other labour organizations. Sergeant Waugh and Corporal Zaneth insinuated themselves into various labour and socialist movements in order to report on the activities of their members. (Throughout the period under discussion in this book the Mounted Police had agents at work as spies in labour unions, political parties and groups such as that connected with the march of the unemployed on Ottawa in 1935. This activity was, in fact, unnecessary and constitutes a shabby chapter in the history of that force.)

The leading figures in the OBU were, for the most part, Britons who had come to Canada in the flood of immigrants at the turn of the century. They had learned their socialism from such British socialists as Henry Hyndman and Robert Blatchford. Despite the vigour of their language—and many were accomplished orators—they were democrats who believed that only by working for the radical reform of existing institutions could they achieve that justice which democracy promised for all. They were more radical than the farmers, not because they had less to lose, but because they had more to gain. Unlike the farmers, they did not even have the satisfaction of being producers. Bodies at the working end of a pick or shovel, hands on the green chain in the mill or at the rock face in the mine—all they had was their self-respect, and that had been severely battered. In common with all trade unionists, their one weapon was the strike. For the OBU the ultimate weapon was the general strike in which all industry and services were shut down.

THE WINNIPEG GENERAL STRIKE

At the Calgary convention the OBU had threatened to call a general strike if certain of its demands were not met, notably the implementation of the six-hour day and the five-day week. Because of this it was assumed at the time (and has been by some writers since) that the Winnipeg general strike was led by the OBU. But, since the OBU had been formed only one month before the Winnipeg strike, it would be unrealistic to credit its organizers with such skills. The fact that many of the leading figures at the Calgary conference were also key men in the strike proves only that the leaders of the Winnipeg labour movement were behind the idea of the OBU.

On May 1, 1919, the workers in the building and metal trades in Winnipeg went out on strike for better wages and union recognition. The wage question was a general one for all workers in the city because of the soaring cost of living. The Winnipeg Trades and Labour Council ordered a vote among its affiliated unions on the question of a general strike in support of the walkout. The result was an overwhelming majority in favour of a general strike, and on May 15 some 30,000 employees walked off their jobs—including some 12,000 who were not even union members. The strike lasted forty-two days. The determination of the strikers to persist was strengthened by the fact that many returned soldiers supported the strike. Until the final days it was free from violence and constituted a remarkable, orderly demonstration of labour solidarity. It showed as well the extent of community dependence upon the members of trade unions.

Initially the Winnipeg strike included suppliers of essential goods and services, such as milk, bread and water. But the Central Strike Committee quickly realized that such services could not be suspended, and consequently they were maintained. Thereafter, milk and bread delivery wagons displayed a placard that read, "By Permission of the Strike Committee." Although the members of the police force voted to strike, the Committee advised them also to stay on the job.

When those opposed to the strike saw the city paralyzed and their own businesses idle, they gave way to all manner of fears and delusions. The most prevalent was that the strike constituted the first of a series of strikes across the country designed to duplicate the Russian Revolution of 1917.

The Winnipeg *Citizen*, a newspaper published during the strike by a committee representing the employers, saw the walkout this way:

> It is to the general public of Winnipeg that we speak in stating without equivocation that this is not a strike in the ordinary sense of the term—it is revolution.

> It is a serious attempt to overturn British institutions in this western country and to supplant them with the Russian Bolshevik system of soviet rule . . . .[3]

Other newspapers, farther from the scene and not directly involved, were no less ready to see in the strike the extension to Canada of the recent Russian Revolution. The Victoria *Daily Colonist*, for example, pointed out that in its fight against "Bolshevism" Winnipeg had to contend with a great many "aliens" who were sympathetic to the Red cause.[4]

There were "sympathetic" strikes in a number of Canadian cities. The most effective was in Vancouver where between 12 and 16 thousand workers went out for thirty days. The sympathy strikes helped to convince many that they were witnessing the unfolding of a nation-wide revolutionary plot. In fact, it was a simple demonstration of labour solidarity. The Strike Committee was seen as a cell of plotting Bolsheviks out to "sovietize" the nation. Otherwise sensible people, who had previously been unaware of their dependence on the working class and ignorant of the nature of such people, feared violence. Many people slept in the churches during the early days of the strike, fearful of being murdered if they spent the night in their homes. The leaders of the strike, however, were conscious of their responsibility and determined to avoid any violence. They constantly urged the strikers to stay home or go fishing, and deliberately avoided marches and mass meetings.

Violence did come toward the end of the strike as a result of the general hysteria that affected the leaders of the anti-strike Citizens Committee. They grew increasingly shrill in their demands that the "insurrection" be put down and the "bohunks," "aliens" and "foreigners" who had plotted the whole thing be jailed. The government supported the anti-strike forces. Troops were sent to Winnipeg and a "citizens' militia" was enrolled. The leaders of the strike were determined to maintain a solid front and avoid violence, but intervention with armed force by the federal government made the likelihood of violence greater. Acting on the "revolutionary plot" theory, the federal government amended the Criminal Code to enable the arrest and deportation, without hearing or trial, of "aliens" suspected of acting with seditious intent.

The stage was set for violence when, contrary to the advice of the strike leaders—those of them who had not been arrested earlier on charges of seditious conspiracy—the returned servicemen organized a "silent march" on the Manitoba legislature to request a report on government efforts to settle the strike. The Mayor of Winnipeg read the riot act; mounted policemen and "specials" armed with baseball bats charged the crowd. When the mêlée that followed was over, one man was dead, another was mortally wounded and thirty were injured.

The Honourable N. W. Rowell, federal Minister of Health, reported to the House of Commons:

> . . . the first shots were fired by the paraders, or those associated with them, and the Mounted Police fired only in self-defence. The information that we have is that the police acted with great coolness, great courage, and great patience . . . . [5]

The *Western Labor News*, a paper that supported the strike, saw the event this way:

> On Saturday about 2:30 P.M., just the time when the parade was scheduled to start, some fifty mounted men swinging baseball bats rode down Main Street. Half were red-coated Royal North-West Mounted Police, the others wore khaki. They quickened their pace as they passed the Union Bank. The crowd opened, let them through and closed in behind them. They turned and charged through the crowd again, greeted by hisses and boos, and some stones. There were two riderless horses with the squad when it emerged and galloped up Main Street. The men in khaki disappeared at this juncture, but the red-coats reined their horses and reformed opposite the old post-office.

"On Saturday about 2:30 P.M., just the time when the parade was scheduled to start, some fifty mounted men swinging baseball bats rode down Main Street. . . ."

" . . . They quickened their pace as they passed the Union Bank. . . ."

Then, with revolvers drawn, they galloped down Main Street, and charged into the crowd on William Avenue, firing as they charged. One man, standing on the sidewalk, thought the mounties were firing blank cartridges until a spectator standing beside him dropped with a bullet through his breast. Another, standing nearby, was shot through the head . . . .[6]

The report went on to point out that had the returned servicemen been prepared for violence, they would hardly have invited their wives to accompany them in their silent parade.

The Winnipeg strike ended July 3 in defeat for the strikers. The intervention of the federal government had been decisive.

The Report of the Robson Committee on the causes of the strike endorsed the contention of the Winnipeg Trades and Labour Council that the high cost of living, long hours, low wages, poor working conditions, profiteering, the refusal of employers to recognize the right of collective bargaining, and the growing awareness of the working class of the inequalities of modern society, were the real causes of the strike. Yet, despite the findings of the Robson Report and the fact that in all the police raids no firearms had been discovered, many believed and some still believe the strike was the start of a Bolshevik revolution in Canada.

In his study the Canadian historian, D. C. Masters, concludes that the strike was not an unsuccessful attempt at revolution;[7] other historians support this conclusion with varying degrees of enthusiasm. There is no evidence to support any other conclusion. Another historian, Kenneth McNaught, argues in his biography of Woodsworth that the great "Red Scare" of 1919 was, in fact, a reflection of the fear that "unionization would get out of hand and kill the golden prospects of profit in a country newly equipped with industrial resources."[8] He goes on to suggest:

> If the country could be convinced that aggressive demands on the part of labour were invariably to be taken as evidence of Bolshevist agitation, the position of the employer of labour in this difficult period would be a good deal more secure.

In the House of Commons at the time, both C. G. Power and Ernest Lapointe suggested the same analysis.

The strike was broken, but its leaders became martyrs in the cause of radical labour action. Although the metal trades did grant collective bargaining, there remained a legacy of resentment over the refusal of legally constituted authority to recognize collective bargaining as a *right*. In addition, many of those active in the leadership of the strikers came to the obvious conclusion that without direct political action little could be achieved toward solving the problems of increasing unemployment, shortage of housing, and the obvious maldistribution of wealth. Just as the farmers had learned that their interests were ignored or misunderstood by the leaders of the "old line" parties, so too labour came to the same conclusion. But it was a long time before unions as such actively invaded the political arena, although individual members did take the plunge.

The OBU flourished briefly after the Winnipeg strike, then gradually declined, giving way to the large international unions, many of which benefited from employers' opposition to the OBU. The distinguishing mark of trade unionism after the 1920's was conservatism. In keeping with the tradition established by Samuel Gompers of the American Federation of Labour, Canadian unions were slow to engage in direct political action through a particular party. What gains they won they were anxious to preserve and consolidate. The radicals found it more to their taste to participate in a political party separate entirely from trade union activity.

THE EMERGENCE OF ORGANIZED FARM PROTEST

During the Winnipeg strike no effort was made to enlist the support of the farmers' groups. It is difficult to say whether the strikers would have had any success had they done so, for the farmers were, by and large, unsympathetic. As a result of the walkout farmers were unable to sell as much of their produce as before, and they considered demands for a six-hour day as sheer laziness bordering on the absurd. Moreover, despite their own stated support for the principle of co-operation and their opposition to the capitalist system, farmers were property owners and viewed with distaste—if not alarm—any real or apparent threats to property rights. *The Grain Growers' Guide*, for example, attacked the strikers for preaching "the doctrines of Bolshevism, confiscation and rule by force."[9] In general, there was never close co-operation between farm and labour in Manitoba. In Saskatchewan and Alberta, where the farmers were more numerous and economically more significant than the labour force, there was more contact and co-operation.

The farmers were not, however, any less strident than labour in their criticism of the "system" and its evil effects on their interests. Some of the most radical statements came from those associated with the Non-Partisan League, an agrarian protest movement that originated in North Dakota. *The Grain Growers' Guide* had championed the cause of a third party for farmers for some time and consequently reported with great glee the victory of the Non-Partisan League in the 1916 state election in North Dakota. The way seemed clear for similar successes in Canada. The Canadian Council of Agriculture was also encouraged by the League's victory, and in December, 1916 it published the "Farmers' Platform."[10] The Platform included demands for tariff reduction, tax reforms and public ownership of all transportation and communication companies, as well as a broad series of political reforms. The real significance of the Platform lay in the fact that it paved the way for political action by the farmers, for although it did not endorse the idea of a third party, obviously neither of the existing parties would endorse all the proposals.

The "Farmers' Platform" went a long way toward helping the Non-Partisan League in its organizational activities in Saskatchewan and Alberta. Characteristic of the League's approach was a strident class consciousness and a broader demand for public ownership than that presented by the Council of Agriculture. Specifically, the League supported public ownership of such vital services to farmers as grain elevators, flour mills and processing plants. The League organizers and its publications were critical of the cabinet system of government, which they claimed perpetuated party rivalry. The system they championed was "business government," in which the legislature would deal with public business objectively, without recourse to partisan debate. They believed this system would ensure that the laws enacted would be the most sound, not merely those that had the support of all the Liberals or all the Conservatives.

Although the Non-Partisan League fared poorly in the Alberta and Saskatchewan provincial elections of 1917, it played a vital role in stimulating both the class consciousness of the farmer and his determination to take the next logical step—direct political action.

The arguments of the League organizers—people like J. S. Woodsworth, William Irvine and Fred Dixon—served to strengthen the anti-party sentiments of the grain growers. They blamed the party system for the failure of the government to meet the demands of the rural population. In 1920, for example, William Irvine published *The Farmers in Politics*, in which he advanced this analysis of the rise of "partyism":

> The ancient principle which justified the birth of the parties gradually weakened and gave place to partyism which ultimately became a sort of fetish to which people blindly and rigidly adhered. When principle was lost, partyism had to resort to other means of sustaining itself. When there was no real national issue, false issues had to be created merely for election purposes; corruption crept in to an alarming degree; graft and patronage eventually were considered as a matter of course, indispensable to the party system; political campaigns grew more expensive, and in consequence the parties became the tools of the wealthy. In fact it may be said that partyism became an investment for big interests in Canada, dividends being paid in the shape of legislation and privileges to those in a position financially and morally to make the investment. Business interests no longer content themselves with financing one of the parties—they donate freely to the campaign funds of both, and so make doubly sure of purchasing government influence, no matter which party happens to be elected. Thus our government machinery has grown to be the most farcical of institutions, being used by the wealthy as a means of attaining financial advancement, and applied to the masses for the purpose of dividing them foolishly against themselves, dividing them in fact to such an extent as to render them politically helpless.[11]

Although the case was clearly overstated, it appealed to the farmers and encouraged the efforts of their leaders to build a movement based on opposition to the party system.

The leading advocate of an alternative to "partyism" was Henry Wise Wood, who proposed the policy of group government. Wood was an American who came to Alberta in 1905 when he was 45 years old. He had already participated in the formation of several American farmers' groups. In 1915 he became vice-president of the United Farmers of Alberta. Professor Morton points out:

> He brought to that office not only the accidental quality of a personality of great force, but a large body of experience in agrarian organization and politics, and a body of ideas distilled from that experience.[12]

Wood's philosophy was simple and direct. Society was made up of several economic groups, of which the farmers were one— and, of course, the largest in the prairie provinces. The party system ignored the significance of these groups and failed to give them adequate representation. Bad government and hardship were the results. The solution was the establishment of a system of government in which the law-making process was carried out, not by opposing parties, but by co-operating groups. The laws passed would then reflect that which all agreed was best for all, and not what one party with a majority could push through against the opposition of the other party. True democracy demanded that parliament consist, not of representatives of the political parties, but of the economic groups into which society is naturally divided.

This philosophy appealed to the farmers for it related government to their own experience. Farmers did not need a two-party system to tell them that frost was bad for crops or which seed was best for spring wheat. They needed only sensible, non-partisan advice; and that was also what the legislators ought to provide the government. There was no need for an opposition party. Competition was as injurious in politics as it was in the economy; co-operation was not only more sensible, it was more Christian. For the farmer, the help he got from, and gave to, his neighbour was an essential aspect of his life. There was no reason that he could see which prevented the same principle being applied in government.

Wood's biographer, W. K. Rolph, wrote:

> Although Wood was accused of being a "Red", a supporter of Marxism, and a dangerous agrarian radical seeking to overthrow the Canadian system of government, he was in fact a conservative, anxious to keep the farmers together and using his influence to prevent the adoption of radical financial, political, or wheat marketing policies which would alienate the more moderate supporters of the farmers' revolt. Cooperation was not only the key to the organization of a successful agrarian movement, but the basis of relations between the farmers and other groups in the state. Throughout his speeches on group action and cooperative marketing runs the idea of unity among all classes in the community as the most satisfactory way to solve all agrarian problems.[13]

The irony of Wood's career is that despite his opposition to party politics and his opposition to class antagonism, his successor as president of the United Farmers of Alberta led that group into affiliation with the CCF in 1932—an act Wood had opposed, but one which his success in organizing the UFA made inevitable.

By 1919, 75,000 prairie farmers were enrolled as members of one of the farmers' organizations. Virtually all supported the "Farmers' Platform". In 1920 the farmers' representatives in the House of Commons, led by T. A. Crerar, decided to constitute themselves as the "National Progressive Party." The creation of this group provided the movement with a national focus and, by implication, an aim: the formation of a national government—although this was never explicitly stated. In December the Canadian Council of Agriculture endorsed the parliamentary group as representative of the farmers' movement and recommended Crerar as leader. In the following year this decision was endorsed by the affiliated farmers' groups. The Progressive party had been born.

The party came into being when times were becoming bad for the farmer. The fat years of the postwar boom were over and the price of wheat was beginning to fall. Between 1920 and 1921 it fell by 40 percent. The fact that there was no equivalent fall in the cost of the goods the farmers had to buy meant severe hardship for many.

The political activity of the farmers became more determined and began to pay off. In 1920 fourteen farmer candidates were elected. In 1921 the UFA became the government of Alberta and in December, 1921, sixty-five Progressive party candidates were elected to the federal parliament, where they constituted the second largest group. This was the first major achievement of the farmers' protest organizations at the national level. It was not their last but it was to remain the most spectacular, short lived though it turned out to be.

*　　*　　*

The end of World War I brought Canada into the industrial era and saw the growth of an urban working class that was beginning to recognise both the need for more adequate representation in the processes of business and industry, and for better representation of their interests in the corridors of government. The trade unions were developing so as to fill both these requirements. In the case of the first, the major battle was to secure employer recognition of the right of collective bargaining; this campaign was not won until the thirties. Labour's role in politics, however, was unclear because union leaders were hesitant, influenced by the conservative view that unions should not play political favourites, but should instead support whichever party was most sympathetic to them. In addition, the unions were divided from within. But with time, as the size and strength of unions grew, a realization of their political potential encouraged union leaders and members to become more active politically.

As an economic group the farmers became more active far sooner than labour. They had had more time to develop a political consciousness and, in addition, had never lacked conviction about the significance of their role in the nation's welfare. Before the second decade of the century had passed, the farmers' groups were deeply involved in political action. Where they could co-operate with the urban labour groups, they did; but initially they engaged in the struggle on their own, as a powerful, united front of outraged producers, determined to win their rights and, at the same time, to reform the system that had clearly led to their state of discontent and deprivation.

The unity of the farmers did not last, for beneath the surface there were fissures of disagreement. But while it lasted the sudden arrival of the farmers' political movement, the Progressive Party, jarred many old time politicians to the very marrow.

Chapter III

The Progressives

The Progressives entered the campaign of 1921 with considerable enthusiasm. True to their philosophical origins, they did not campaign as a national party, although their leader, T. A. Crerar, did tour most of Canada. Instead, they campaigned almost exclusively in individual constituencies. Each electoral district was an autonomous unit in the party and as a result there was neither a national campaign nor an overall campaign strategy.

A national campaign would have been rather awkward, for there was a split within the movement. It was not serious in the beginning, but as the Progressives edged further into politics it grew and deepened. The division was between the Alberta wing and the Manitoba wing or, more specifically, between Crerar and Henry Wise Wood. Crerar saw the election as an opportunity to bring the Liberal party to its senses, and to force a tariff reduction and free trade in agricultural products. He was not fundamentally opposed to the party system. He had been in the Borden cabinet and was no stranger to cabinet solidarity and party discipline. Wood, understandably, said of the 1921 election:

> The issue is between the old party system and the system we have built up.[1]

Progressives of his persuasion characterised the old system as the tool by which the big interests had corrupted the electorate and had run the country to serve their own selfish ends.

A further bone of contention was the question of free trade versus government control in the marketing of grain. During the war the federal government had assumed control of the marketing of wheat. A board was established that fixed the price of wheat and controlled the marketing of the crops in 1917

29

W. L. Mackenzie King, a prime minister sensitive to the shifting political winds in western Canada.

and 1918. In 1919 the Canadian Wheat Board was set up to handle the selling of that year's crop, but the legislation was not renewed for 1920. The Manitoba wing of the Progressives was more interested in free trade and not much concerned about the demise of the wheat board. The Saskatchewan farmers, on the other hand, were well pleased with the effects of the wheat board and wanted to see the federal government stay in the business of marketing wheat. They believed this policy would result in stable prices and secure markets.

Of the two leaders of the "old line parties," as the farmers called them, Mackenzie King of the Liberals was the most shrewd. Prime Minister Arthur Meighen of the Conservatives displayed the short-sighted arrogance that became his trademark in politics and contributed materially to his lack of success. King saw the Progressives as impatient Liberals and attempted to placate the western farmers by telling them things about his tariff policy that he did not dare say in eastern Canada. Meighen either ignored the farmers' demands or referred to them as "Socialistic, Bolshevistic and Soviet nonsense." He described the governments they had formed in Ontario and Alberta as "freaks."

R. B. Bennett: too rich to understand the poor and too proud to admit it.

Meighen and King were campaigning to form a government—they were seeking power. The Progressive did not want power, they merely wanted representation. This fitted well their constituency by constituency campaign. The voters were not asked to elect a Progressive government, they were simply asked to elect a Progressive to represent them in Ottawa—an important distinction.

THE PROGRESSIVES AT OTTAWA

The election of sixty-five Progressives might appear to be a great start for a party but the results were actually a disappointment. Only one Progressive was elected east of the Ottawa river; the majority were from the prairies, with twenty-four from Ontario and five from British Columbia. They constituted a western block dedicated to the interests of the wheat farmer.

Although his party was the largest group in the House of Commons, Mackenzie King did not have a majority. Soon after the election he set about to bring the Progressives into some sort of alliance. The Progressives viewed his advances with mixed feelings. The Alberta wing, strongly committed to the idea of constituency autonomy and opposed to party politics, condemned any arrangement with the Liberals. The Manitoba wing wanted only to reform the Liberal party and would have entered into some agreement without much difficulty. But King did not have complete unanimity in his own party. The conservative wing represented by Sir Lomer Gouin and his Quebec colleagues, despised Progressivism and opposed any alliance.

King first offered cabinet representation to the Progressives in return for some kind of coalition arrangement. The offer was ultimately denied by King and, in any case, it was turned down by the Progressives. As a result of the reticence of the Albertans, the most the Progressives would agree to was conditional support of the Liberals. They recognized that there was likely to be more for them to support in the program of a Liberal administration than in that of the Conservatives.

In the discussions that took place before the opening of the new parliament, the division in the ranks of the radicals was evident. Crerar, as an experienced parliamentarian, was concerned about establishing the machinery of parliamentary discipline to ensure that the Progressives voted as a single unit, as a party, in fact. This involved the institution of a caucus, party whip and reasonable adherence to the direction of the parliamentary leaders. The Alberta Progressives opposed this approach, for they saw themselves as spokesmen for their constituents not as subordinate members of a political party. Despite his efforts and conditional agreement from his followers, Crerar never achieved the kind of solidarity necessary to enable the Progressives to operate effectively in a parliamentary setting.

Although they were the second largest group in parliament, the Progressives did not choose to form the official opposition. This right they yielded to Meighen's Conservatives. The Progressives did not see themselves as an alternative government. They were a kind of pressure group, sitting in parliament to chastise the unfeeling and to assist those who wanted to help the farmers. By refusing responsibility and, by implication, demonstrating their lack of interest in forming a government, they made it possible for other politicians and the rest of the country to refuse to take them seriously. They rejected the opportunity to achieve the cohesion they so desperately needed to reach their goals.

The Progressives could not become the official opposition because of their principles. The Manitoba Progressives did not want to oppose the Liberals—they only wanted to reform them. The Alberta Progressives did not want to engage in the competitive processes of party government—they wanted to eradicate party government. For opposite reasons, therefore, the two wings of the Progressive group combined to pass up a chance to become a political party.

The Progressives were determined to demonstrate that they were an independent body, free to support the government or to oppose it in the light of their principles and the needs of their constituents. As Professor Morton has remarked:

> It was a brave experiment, inspired by political naiveté, and marked by a curious over-emphasis on the importance of legislation and an ill-advised indifference to the importance of administration.[2]

It was a difficult position for the group to maintain, particularly as they lacked the unity such a role demanded. They were, in Morton's phrase, a "restive and unreliable band." Mackenzie King could count on Progressive support, however, for as much as the westerners disliked the Liberals, they liked the Conservatives even less.

> Only the Albertan Progressives could regard the two old parties as indifferently steeped in iniquity.[3]

The rules of the House of Commons at that time were designed to facilitate the operation of a two-party parliament, composed of government and opposition. The Progressives did not fit the pattern. Because of the rules of the Commons, they found themselves unable to move a sub-amendment to the Conservative amendment to the government's budget. Thus they were deprived of a prime opportunity to criticise government fiscal policy, their chief concern at the time. Unable to get their own proposals before the House, they were forced to vote with the Conservatives. Their most significant achievement in the

1922 session was in gaining the government's agreement to reinstate the 1918 Crowsnest Pass rates on the shipment of grain and flour—to the advantage of the farmer.

TENSION AND DISINTEGRATION

By the end of 1922 cracks in the Progressive ranks were widening. Two Progressives slipped away to become Liberals. Crerar tried toward the end of the parliamentary session to bring his group closer to the Liberals by proposing some kind of working agreement between the two. The proposal was turned down and Crerar resigned as leader, to be replaced by Robert Forke. Forke was no less liberal than Crerar. His initial actions were toward establishing a national Progressive *party*. This move was opposed by the Alberta members and failed to succeed. Forke's failure in this regard—really the failure of the Progressives—marked the beginning of the end. There was nothing for them to do.

The two views on the movement's purpose turned the Progressives into a body of dissidents, in danger of disintegration. The Alberta view of the Member of Parliament as a delegate was simply inconsistent with the structure of parliament. The views of the Manitoba moderates were inconsistent with the radical strain in Progressive thought. Progressivism began to disintegrate through the centrifugal forces generated by the inconsistency and contradiction in its doctrine and composition.

In 1923 the Conservative party allowed the Progressives to make the major amendment to the budget motion. Forke made a frontal assault on Liberal tariff policy, calling for a reduction in the tariff on the necessities of life, more favourable terms of trade with Britain, reciprocity in trade with the United States and increased taxation on unearned incomes and luxury items. The ringing presentation of the bare bones of their policy united the Progressives as never before. The combination of the Progressive and Conservative assault on the Liberal budget reduced King's combined majority to 8. This was the Progressives' finest hour. Their course was downhill thereafter. In particular, they were beaten to a standstill in their attempt to amend the Bank Act in 1923—although some of the reforms they advocated were later enacted.

The major break in Progressive ranks occurred in 1924.

During the debate on the budget of that session, J. S. Woodsworth, Labour MP from Winnipeg North, moved an amendment that was substantially the same as that moved by Forke the previous year. The Progressives were in a difficult position. If they supported Woodsworth's amendment, the Liberal government could conceivably be defeated. If they opposed it, they would be repudiating their own principles. One of the main criticisms the Progressives made of the old parties was that they seldom stood by their principles.

Forke led most of his followers in opposition to Woodsworth's amendment on the grounds that there was more likelihood of a Liberal government enacting Progressive reforms than would ever be the case with the Conservatives. To defeat the government would, then, be folly. Fourteen Progressives disagreed and supported the Woodsworth amendment. As E. J. Garland of the breakaway group of Progressives declared on the floor of the House, his constituents would be:

> ... encouraged to know that even though our efforts are largely nullified by the attitudes of opposing interests, they have at least representatives who are pleading their cause without fear of party or press, and who will not be silent while injustice still stands.[4]

Six of the fourteen renegades left the Progressive party shortly after, constituting what became known as the "Ginger Group." In an open letter to Robert Forke they said:

> As we see it there are two species of political organization—one the 'Political Party' that aspires to power, and in so doing, inevitably perpetuates that competitive spirit in matters of legislation and government generally which has brought the world wellnigh to ruin; the other is the democratically organized group which aims to co-operate with other groups to secure justice rather than to compete with them for power. It is as representatives of this latter type that we take our stand .....[5]

The Ginger Group was later joined by three more Progressives.

By 1925 the Progressive party was shattered beyond repair. Seventeen broke with the caucus and voted with the Liberals on the 1925 budget. When the election was called that year there was little to hold the group together. They had no funds and no national organization. Only 24 Progressive MP's were left when the votes had been counted. The Conservatives under Meighen had the most seats this time, but not a clear majority.

In the constitutional crises which followed, the Progressives played the part of makeweight and were responsible first for the defeat of King's administration and finally for the defeat of Arthur Meighen's. In the 1926 election Liberals and Progressives reached an agreement not to oppose one another in several ridings; in others "Liberal-Progressives" appeared. When the 1926 session of parliament opened there were only nine "pure" Progressives left.

THE LESSON OF PROGRESSIVE EXPERIENCE

To some extent the Progressives had achieved their goals. The eastern politicians and magnates had been jolted into an awareness of the needs of the farmers, even if these demands were not entirely met. The general spirit of reform, which had fostered the farmers' movements and had led to the creation of the Progressive party, had achieved some results in increasing the amount of social welfare legislation at the provincial level. But prosperity helped to take some of the steam from the movement, and the manifest failure of the party in parliament aided the process of diminution. Third parties, it seemed, had no place in the context of parliamentary government, and if they could not effect changes in the rules—as the Progressives had tried and failed to do—then they remained both vulnerable and impotent. This factor and the concessions Mackenzie King made to the west in the election of 1926, effectively brought an end to the career of the Progressive party. The Liberal-Progressives in the House of Commons insisted on keeping their dual identity but they attended the Liberal caucus and were seated in the House with the Liberals. Slowly but surely they were absorbed and digested by the Liberals.

The left-overs—those who sat as UFA members or Independent Progressives—were themselves absorbed in a different way by a different group. When the Progressives flared into prominence in the 1921 election, two Labour MP's were also elected:

J. S. Woodsworth for Winnipeg North Centre and William Irvine for East Calgary. By 1923 Woodsworth had established his right to speak after Robert Forke as the leader of a party. Earlier Irvine had referred in debate to the presence of a "Labour Group" in the Commons; "Mr. Woodsworth is the leader," he said, "and I am the group." [6]

The Labour group had met occasionally with the more radical of the Progressives. After the Ginger Group had separated itself from the decaying carcass of the Progressive party, meetings of this group with the Labour group were more frequent and collaboration was the rule rather than the exception. By 1930 co-operation had proceeded to the stage that more formal arrangements could be considered. A document was drawn up which stated that the groups were "engaged in the common fight against a strongly entrenched system of special privilege," and affirmed the decision to work in unison to develop "a co-operative system of administration."[7] Each group was to retain its identity, and there was no intention to form another political party. A steering committee was elected, a secretary appointed, and a chairman was elected to act on behalf of all the groups in the event that there was insufficient time for a conference. In effect, therefore, the document did lay the groundwork for a political party. Two years later the "co-operating groups" were to agree to begin building a new political party.

Much had happened between 1926 and 1932 to convince J. S. Woodsworth and his colleagues in the House of Commons that there was enough support in the country to spell success for another organized attempt to break the two party monopoly. The onset of the depression and a series of crop failures once again brought the farmer up against the precarious nature of his occupation. There had been increased activity on the part of the various labour and socialist parties in the cities in the west. The failure of the Progressive party had certainly dampened the political ambitions of the farmers' organizations, but they had not disappeared.

What the Progressive experience had shown was the impossibility of effective parliamentary action by a loosely linked body of independents. The Progressives had assumed that government was essentially the process of law-making and that as long as you had a seat or two in the House of Commons you could have a voice in making the laws. They had not understood the mechanism of parliament, nor had they realized that the centre of power was the executive, not the legislature.

The cabinet governs the country through the civil service, and cabinets are only interested in parties other than their own if those parties constitute a threat in the House of Commons. Had the Progressives been a single, united party, and had they been willing to play the parliamentary game with the Conservatives, they could have forced Mackenzie King to do more for the farmers—by threatening to defeat his government. But they had not been united and could never have been because the Alberta group at least, and certainly several from the other provinces, had championed the view that the Member of Parliament ought not to be subordinate to the party. They had held that his first duty was to his constituents and his principles. It would have been odd, indeed, if having been elected because they opposed "partyism" the Progressives had turned around and adopted it.

If everyone playing a game follows one set of rules, those who join under their own different rules soon discover they have no hope of achieving any of their goals. It did not matter how valid the cause of the Progressives was, nor how accurate their criticism of the "old line" parties; they achieved little because they had not played the party game.

The Progressives had erred in thinking that it was parliament and the party system that were at fault and causing their trouble. To some extent the influence of American reform ideas and American experience had led to this misapprehension, for in the American Congress the individual member does have more influence than his counterpart in the Canadian House of Commons. Leadership in the Canadian House lies with the cabinet. Members, in effect, merely approve cabinet proposals or oppose them. The cabinet retains its right to lead the Commons and govern the country by virtue of the support it has in the House of Commons. Generally, this support is guaranteed because the prime minister and his cabinet colleagues are the leaders of the majority party in the Commons and that party, through strict party discipline, votes as a bloc. The addition of sixty-five undisciplined Progressives had alerted the Liberal and Conservative parties to the discontent of the farmers, but it did not force the government to make the concessions the Progressives had assumed their victory would bring.

*   *   *

When the CCF was established it appeared the lesson of the Progressive experience had been learned. Unlike the Progressives, the CCF was a vigorous champion of the parliamentary system and its members became particularly adept in using the institution to achieve the goals of the socialist movement. Social Credit, on the other hand, never demonstrated any great fondness for the institution, and on more than one occasion its members indicated that they considered it a nuisance. J. S. Woodsworth, M. J. Coldwell and Stanley Knowles of the CCF were all, at various times, described as great parliamentarians. William Aberhart of the Social Credit party rarely spoke in the Alberta legislature and W. A. C. Bennett of the B.C. Social Credit party considered that there was altogether too much talk in the chamber.

From the Progressive experience in the twenties and the agrarian opposition to "partyism", these two strands, the CCF and Social Credit, branch off, each running in different directions from the same source. In neither case was the position of the Member of Parliament—or of the provincial legislator—reconsidered in the light of Progressive ideas. For the CCF, the MP remained a representative and a party member; for the Social Credit party, he was an adjunct to the cabinet and the civil service, with a much more reduced role in the legislative process than even the normal parliamentary system envisaged. The Progressive ideal of members as delegates from their constituencies or from their economic groups languished and died, killed by the necessity of party unity that the cabinet system of parliamentary government demanded.

Chapter IV

The Great Depression

The depression of the 1930's dealt a particularly severe blow to Canada because the Canadian economy was especially vulnerable to fluctuations in the international economy and was then, as now, closely tied to the American economy. During the period from roughly 1900 to 1930, the Canadian economy was expanding. The rate of growth was not steady, there being slumps and serious dislocation in various sectors during this period; but overall the picture was one of expansion and general prosperity.

THE ECONOMIC BACKGROUND

Prosperity before the depression was not spread equally across the country amongst all Canadians. While the economy boomed, however, there was little concern expressed for those whose share of the nation's wealth was barely sufficient to sustain even the most basic standard of living. The needy were not entirely ignored, but the attitude of some persons toward the problem of poverty was curious, as J. S. Woodsworth indicated in the House of Commons in 1931 when he read the following advertisement from a newspaper:

> Here's the sort of philanthropy you've dreamed about— the sort that will cost you next to nothing. It will increase your self-respect in more ways than one—and it may mean a job for an unemployed man—at least it will keep him warm. Buy yourself a new suit—give your old suit to the unemployed. What you discard is a luxury to the man in tatters. It will increase his self-respect too. Think of the chap who has to shovel snow to tide him over to the next job in his trade.[1]

The next job in his trade was unlikely to do much to enable the man to buy a new suit like his benefactor; wages were low and working conditions poor. Wages fell even lower during the depression, as the evidence gathered in 1934 by a royal commission investigating price spreads indicated:

> Male piece-workers in one large Montreal factory averaged 16 cents per hour, less than the minimum of 18 cents for inexperienced females. One man of ten years' experience worked 70 hours per week in a Montreal contract shop, to earn $7 at 10 cents per hour. In one Montreal factory, all workers, men and women together, averaged 25 cents per hour. In 1932, out of 115 men in two thoroughly good Toronto union shops, 57 earned for the year less than $800; 88 less than $1000; only 27 earned over $1000; and only 2 over $1600.

> Hours of employment are often oppressively long. Thirteen hours a day, 60 hours a week, are not uncommon in rush periods.[2]

When the depression occurred, it merely deepened the misery for many, while introducing others to it for the first time.

Canadians had geared their economy to the production of goods for foreign markets, in particular the provision of foodstuffs, newsprint, lumber and minerals. The production of these commodities required the construction of a huge transportation system, processing plants and a considerable investment in implements and machinery. To finance these projects money was borrowed from other countries, primarily from Britain and the United States. As long as there was a steady demand for these products the Canadian economy prospered and the rather narrow specialization in the production of raw materials and foodstuffs paid off. But when the overseas market slumped, the effect was immediately felt in Canada and was disastrous. If, for example, the price of newsprint dropped, income was insufficient to pay off the money borrowed to build the papermill, and workers were laid off. Less was then spent on the products of secondary industry, more people were thrown out of work, and the descent into slump or depression began.

"Buddy, can you spare a dime?" (the title of a popular song in the 1930's).

Farmers had already experienced the effects of a drop in the price of wheat. Although they were getting less money for their grain, they still had to make the same payments for the implements, seed and land they had bought. Consequently they found themselves being squeezed between the nether millstone of low prices for their products and the upper millstone of high payments for their machinery and land.

When the world depression began, with the collapse of the New York stock market in 1929 heralding the collapse of the international economy, the effects soon became apparent in Canada. Operating on the assumption that the world economy would remain healthy, Canada was unprepared for what followed. The political, public finance and economic organizations were not adapted to deal with sharp and prolonged reverses. The Rowell-Sirois Commission later pointed out:

> When a specific and co-ordinated program was required, there was bewilderment; when positive action was needed there were only temporizing and negative policies; when a realization of the far-reaching effects of the altered circumstances was demanded, there was but faith in the speedy return to the old conditions of prosperity.[3]

Conditions were aggravated by the fact that Canada was overextended in her production of newsprint and wheat. For example, in 1928 there had been a bumper wheat crop and a world surplus of both products resulting in lower prices. Since Canada supplied 40 percent of the world's wheat and 65 percent of the world's newsprint, she suffered the full impact of overproduction and falling prices in these commodities. Those areas of Canada that depended upon the production of these two commodities for their economic health became grievously ill.

The effects of the depression were not the same across the country. The people most severely affected were those engaged in the production of primary products and those out of work. The average annual income of most people fell, but in Saskatchewan, Alberta, Manitoba and British Columbia it fell drastically. In 1928/29 the average income per person in Saskatchewan was $478. Four years later it was down to $135, a decrease of 71 percent. In Saskatchewan, the province most severely hit by

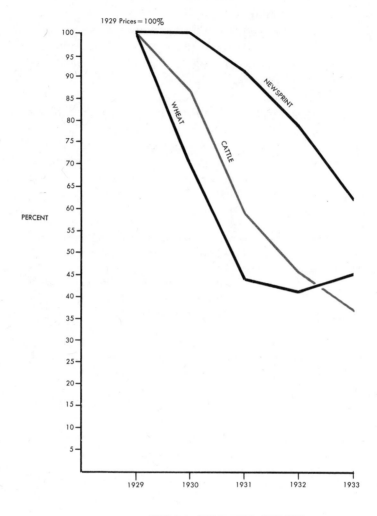

1929 Prices = 100%

PERCENT

NEWSPRINT

WHEAT

CATTLE

DECLINE IN EXPORT PRICES, 1929-1933

the depression, the blow was intensified by a series of crop failures and drought. In 1937 two thirds of the farm population of that province was destitute.

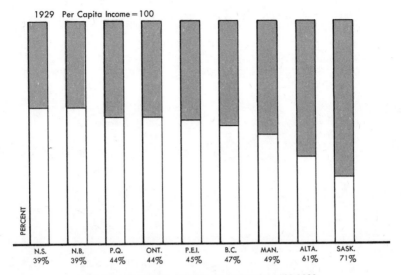

1929 Per Capita Income = 100

PERCENT

| N.S. | N.B. | P.Q. | ONT. | P.E.I. | B.C. | MAN. | ALTA. | SASK. |
| 39% | 39% | 44% | 44% | 45% | 47% | 49% | 61% | 71% |

DECLINE IN PER CAPITA INCOME BY PROVINCE, 1929-1933

One observer of the prairie scene, after a tour through Saskatchewan, wrote in the Regina *Leader Post* in 1934:

> The land was as lifeless as ashes, and for miles there was scarcely a growing thing to be seen. Where a scanty herbage had struggled up through the dust, flights of grasshoppers had apparently completed the destruction . . . .

> And as for the people themselves, God only knows what their extremity must be. One farmer . . . gathered and threshed 400 bushels of wheat from 150 acres*, his oats sown on 30 acres being a complete failure making it necessary to buy oats for both seed and feed—if he can buy them . . . . This man is one of the best farmers in the municipality . . . .[4]

*An average yield would be 25-30 bushels per acre, or 3250-4500 bushels from 150 acres.

A year later the Rev. A. M. Nicholson, who later became a CCF MP and a cabinet minister in the Saskatchewan CCF government, described in his diary the conditions of some farms:

> Thursday, March 28, 1935. Drove from Carragana-Bell's Hill . . . . R-- offered to send one of the family to a neighbour's and let us have the bed . . . . They had no hay or oats for our team. We fortunately had a sack of chop in the cutter. They apologized for their food—moose meat, white bread, tea without sugar or milk. They had no fruit, butter or potatoes.[5]

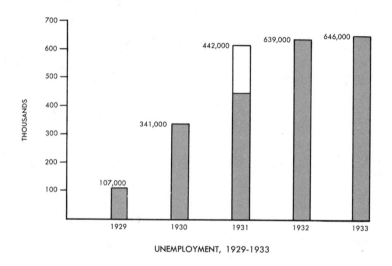

UNEMPLOYMENT, 1929-1933

The situation was only slightly better in Alberta where there had been better luck with crops; but more farmers there had a heavy burden of debt that had to be paid off whether the price of wheat was high or low. In British Columbia and Manitoba unemployment was concentrated in Vancouver and Winnipeg, where the closing down of industries threw hundreds of men out of work. In Vancouver the ranks of the unemployed were swollen by the arrival of men from the lumber camps and mines whose jobs depended upon overseas sales of timber, newsprint and minerals. The more temperate climate of the coast

city attracted unemployed from elsewhere in the country as well
—it was easier to sleep on a park bench there. By 1933 over half
a million Canadian men were out of work.

THE RESPONSE TO DEPRESSION

The federal government, to put it mildly, was unaccustomed to
such widespread dislocation and hardship. Its initial reaction
was to leave the provision of welfare and relief in the hands of
the provinces and municipalities—agencies that were just as
unaccustomed to the role and far less able to deal with the
problems created by the depression. The federal government did
provide most of the funds for relief but with little oversight or
control. Consequently, there were glaring and unjustifiable
variations in the standards of relief available across the country.
Those on relief were subjected to a bewildering array of regulations and to notorious examples of graft and patronage. The
whole situation compounded despair and appeared to be designed
to do anything but alleviate distress.

It would be difficult to exaggerate the human misery
and social dislocation occasioned by the depression in Canada.
For the single unemployed men in the labour camps, life was a
dreary succession of days in which there was little to do but line
up for soup, while enforced idleness slowly corroded all sense of
human dignity. For others it was a series of unsuccessful attempts to earn a dime or two shovelling snow, raking leaves,
selling apples. Some men travelled back and forth across the
country on, in and under freight cars. They were harassed by
railway police, driven from towns by local constables and
generally treated as infectious parasites. Farmers in the west
could not afford gas for their cars, so they hitched them to their
horses and thereby invented the "Bennett Buggy," named after
Prime Minister Bennett whose government inherited the depression and fumbled it badly. When, in 1935, the unemployed in
Vancouver started a trek to Ottawa to demand work and wages,
they were met on the way with some help but mostly hatred.
In Regina, while their leaders were negotiating with Prime
Minister Bennett, the trekkers were, in effect, declared subversive,
and anyone helping them was made subject to arrest under

Mackenzie King tests the riding qualities of a "Bennett Buggy".

section 98 of the Criminal Code. The "on-to-Ottawa trek" ended in a riot in Regina.

Reports of Prime Minister Bennett's response to the trekkers vary. One of the trekkers, Ron Liversedge, wrote an account of the adventure and described the meeting with the Prime Minister:

> There sat Bennett behind his desk, surrounded by officials and guards. There were the press, and in front of Bennett the eight representatives of the trek. The Prime Minister wasted no time, but went into his diatribe of abuse, condemnation, and threats, his face crimson with hatred.
>
> He then singled out Slim Evans, and roared, "We know you down here Evans! You are a criminal and a thief!" At this Slim rose calmly to his feet, and looking the Prime Minister in the eye, he said, loudly and distinctly, "And you're a liar Bennett, and what is more, you are not fit to

run a Hottentot village, let alone a great country like Canada." The delegation was hustled out, and that was our negotiations . . . . [6]

The news report of Bennett's remarks as published in the Vancouver *Province* differed somewhat:

We have taken care of our unemployed as well as any country in the world and in most of these camps content-ment prevails, if not real happiness.

Agitators, representing a form of government we will not tolerate in this country—representing Communism which we will stamp out in Canada—got into these camps to destroy them. You men are the victims of that agitation . . . .

You are now facing those . . . who represent law and order and who propose that law and order shall be maintained in this country. You ask for work and wages. You haven't shown much anxiety to get work. It is the one thing you don't want. What you want is adventure in the hope of over-awing authority and upsetting the government. [7]

The *Province* report is perhaps more accurate than Liversedge's, if not as colourful, but it seems obvious that Prime Minister Bennett was less than sympathetic to the trekkers.

For those already convinced of the inequity—if not, indeed, the iniquity—of the capitalist system, the depression deepened their conviction and spurred their determination to take more direct action. The men and women in the several socialist and labour parties in the west had begun to move toward concerted action as early as 1929. The farmers, many of whom regretted the failure of the Progressive party and were anxious to try again, were joined by others as the fluctuations of the world market and crop conditions revealed once more their vulnerable position.

UNITING FOR THE CO-OPERATIVE COMMONWEALTH

There were many labour and socialist parties in Western Canada at this time, each with a different name and most with their own preferred socialist doctrine. In British Columbia there was a Canadian Labour party and a Socialist Party of Canada. In Alberta there were branches of the Canadian

"Travel now, pay later", on-to-Ottawa trek style.

Labour party and the Dominion Labour party. There was an Independent Labour Party in Saskatchewan and one in Manitoba—the one for which J. S. Woodsworth was MP. In 1929 delegates from these parties and from several trade unions, some of which held radical political views, met in Regina to "correlate the activities of the several labour political parties in western Canada."[8] The Manitoba *Free Press* saw the conference as the beginning of a Western Canadian Labour Party, but it was not quite that. The groups did not amalgamate, they merely passed resolutions of a radical nature and agreed to meet again the following year in Medicine Hat.

The second meeting of what became known as the Conference of Western Labour Political Parties was more radical than the first, and with reason. The effects of the depression were being felt. It was not until the third gathering, in Winnipeg in July of 1931, that delegates undertook to form a national labour party. Several of the farmers' organizations were invited to that conference. It was recognized that the plight of farmers and workers was similar and that from concerted action results satisfactory to both could be achieved. There was no disagreement on policy; the farmers' groups had been moving further from the reformist doctrines of the Progressives toward a more distinctly socialist position. All the delegates at Winnipeg in 1931 agreed that, "capitalism must go and socialism be established."[9] Their aim was the establishment of a "co-operative commonwealth."

Formal steps were to be taken to build the new political movement at the fourth meeting of the Labour Conference. As the labour parties moved closer together, submerging philosophical differences in a common cause, so too the farmers' groups, as they moved leftward, moved together and came to accept more fully the need for direct political action. The decision of the labour parties to unite coincided with a similar decision on the part of the United Farmers of Alberta to invite all groups sharing a faith in the ideal of the co-operative commonwealth to attend a conference in Calgary in 1932.

The United Farmers of Alberta (UFA) had formed the government of Alberta in 1925 but had resisted the call of federal politics, largely because of the anti-party philosophy of their leader, Henry Wise Wood. Wood retired in 1931 and was succeeded by Robert Gardiner, a member of the Ginger Group in the federal House of Commons. Gardiner was determined to put together a national political party and consequently led the UFA to the point where their convention called for the formation of a party to fight for the rights of farmers and workers alike. The co-operative commonwealth they, and the other groups, were seeking was defined as:

> A community freed from the domination of irresponsible financial and economic power, in which all social means of production and distribution, including land, are socially owned and controlled either by voluntarily organized groups of producers and consumers, or ... by public corporations responsible to the peoples' elected representatives.[10]

In Saskatchewan the Independent Labour Party, formed by M. J. Coldwell, a school principal and Regina alderman, had been working with the Farmers' Political Association led by

George Williams. The two had collaborated as the Farmer-Labour party in provincial elections and both groups were active in organizing farmers and workers into local groups of one or other of these organizations. One such group was formed in Weyburn in 1932 by a young Baptist clergyman, T. C. Douglas. That same year the farmers and city workers agreed to present a single joint program and to undertake joint political action, creating in effect a Saskatchewan farmer-labour party, although both groups retained their identity. As the leader of the agrarian side of the new movement put it, the philosophy of the farmer-labour alliance was "fundamentally socialistic."[11]

The Manitoba ILP, with headquarters in Winnipeg and active branches in the smaller towns like Brandon and Souris, assumed responsibility for the development of the movement toward a new political party. The United Farmers of Manitoba were not hostile to the activities of the labour party but were not prepared to officially endorse their activities. Rural Manitoba was more in the Liberal-Progressive tradition and there was less agrarian support for the socialism of the ILP. In Winnipeg itself, however, with its large proportion of industrial workers, many of whom were immigrants, there was a lot of support.

In eastern Canada there was considerable activity among the labour and socialist parties, but it was disorganized and sporadic. There were more than a dozen labour and socialist parties of various colorations in Toronto alone. What organized political activity there was occurred largely through the efforts of the United Farmers of Ontario, a farmers' organization that was closer to the old Progressives in outlook than to the radical UFA or the Saskatchewan Farmers' Political Association. Nevertheless, the presence of these bodies did indicate that a national party of the left might find some support in Ontario.

There was some support in the intellectual community as well. In 1931 two university professors, one from McGill and the other from the University of Toronto, agreed that Canada needed a new political party, one which would not share the fate of the Progressives and be devoured by Mackenzie King's Liberals. The two, Frank Scott and Frank Underhill, established a society to provide such a party with a doctrine that would prove unpalatable to Mr. King. The society was known as the League for Social Reconstruction and soon had branches in Montreal, Toronto, Winnipeg and Vancouver. In many respects it was like the British Fabian Society, and like it hoped to become the intellectual wing of a Canadian socialist party.

The farm and labour MP's in the House of Commons were not unaware of the activities of the farm and labour groups across the country. Woodsworth had attended the conferences of the Western Labour Political Parties, had been in touch with Coldwell and Williams in Saskatchewan, and was honorary president of the League for Social Reconstruction. Robert Gardiner was president of the UFA. Miss Agnes Macphail was in the United Farmers of Ontario. On May 26, 1932, the members of the co-operating groups in the House of Commons met in the office of William Irvine and decided to bring all these strands together in a single political movement, which they tentatively called the "Commonwealth Party." Each member was given specific organizational responsibilities and all were to take every opportunity to organize support for the new party. Each one had, so to speak, grown up in the tradition of radical protest. The fact that they were meeting together as representatives of the farm and labour groups was evidence of a fundamental unity that had always existed but which had required the stress of the depression to become manifest across the land. Each had learned the lessons taught by the failure of the Progressive party and all were determined to avoid these mistakes.

The new venture they were beginning had a considerable advantage over the Progressive movement in that there was one obvious leader in the figure of J. S. Woodsworth. A man of heroic determination and devotion to principle, Woodsworth was accepted by farmer and worker alike as the symbol of the emerging movement. He had been a Methodist minister earlier in his career but had resigned from his church because of its failure to apply the teaching of the gospels to all men, and because of its attitude toward free speech. He had worked as a longshoreman in British Columbia, had travelled through the prairies on behalf of the Non-Partisan League and had edited the *Western Labor News* during the Winnipeg general strike.

In his own actions as well as in his statements on the public platform and in parliament, Woodsworth symbolized the aspirations of the men and women who were working through the farm and labour movements to bring about a better society. He spoke for all these when he moved in the House of Commons the first of what became an annual series of resolutions:

> That in the opinion of this House the government should immediately take measures looking to the setting up of a co-operative commonwealth in which all the natural resources and socially necessary machinery of production will be used in the interest of the people and not for the benefit of the few.[12]

The submerging of political division and animosity in creating a federation of the diverse groups in Calgary in 1932 was a tribute to the symbolic and actual leadership of J. S. Woodsworth. He was subsequently described by a Liberal journalist as "a saint in politics."[13]

Outside the circle of his own followers and those commentators of a fairly liberal outlook, Woodsworth was seen almost as the devil incarnate, corrupting young minds when he spoke to university students, and preaching revolution and totalitarianism in his speeches in the House of Commons. It would have been surprising had the reaction to Woodsworth and his colleagues been anything else, for what they proposed constituted, at that time, a major reallocation of the nation's economic resources—and that was gross interference with the rights of private property.

Those who believed that private property and free enterprise—the capitalist system—formed the basis of individual freedom could not accept the proposals of the socialists despite the evidence of the depression that the system was clearly not working well for all the people. A majority of Canadians believed that socialism was evil and that poverty and unemployment were the result of bad luck or poor management. They were unwilling to accept the arguments of Woodsworth that the economic system was stacked against the many in the interest of the few. Proposals for unemployment insurance were scoffed at as subsidizing laziness; public ownership was said to be a form of theft that led to dictatorship.

It was characteristic of Woodsworth that despite the criticism of his ideas, he persisted when lesser men would have withdrawn from the struggle. As many of his ideas and the policies of the party he helped create were adopted and enacted by the Liberal government, many of his critics recognized the essentially noble character of the man. Pacifist, humanitarian and socialist, he was a key factor in knitting together the various strands that emerged as the fabric of a new political party, the Co-operative Commonwealth Federation or, as it was usually called, the CCF.

*   *   *

The depression, acting as a catalyst, hastened the growth of the CCF but it did not, in the strict sense, cause it. By 1929 radicals in the cities and on the farms had already seen the need for a broader and more united base. The depression served to validate this belief, for it was proof of both the inadequacies of the capitalist economy and the insensitivity of the "old line" parties. Furthermore, despite the prevalence of hardship in western Canada, the depression would not bring immediate victory to the new party in the 1935 election. This was largely because the CCF was very new and, paradoxically, because its "revolutionary" character, in comparison to the other parties, had no direct appeal to those who were down and out. Socialism was to receive its greatest support at a time when prosperity had returned and those enjoying it were prepared to adopt a radical stance in order to retain it. As Professor Lipset has pointed out, support for radical movements on a large scale comes on the flood tide of rising expectations, not on the ebb of desolation and depression.

Woodsworth, Irvine and the Ginger Group had a foothold in parliament. The formation of the CCF gave them the beginnings of a nation-wide organization based on an alliance of what were essentially movements—bodies of like-minded people, dedicated to reform and prepared to make remarkable sacrifices to achieve their goals of social and political reform. As politicians, the leaders of the CCF recognized the need to weld the groups together into a democratic party that would aim for power. As participants in a movement, they could, as well, draw satisfaction from the achievement of any of their goals, whether they were in power themselves or not. In this regard they were soon able to see the results of their efforts as Mackenzie King reacted to their presence and edged his party leftward.

The tragic consequences of the depression and the ineptitude of governments in dealing with it hardened the determination of men like Woodsworth to do their utmost to ensure that it never happened again.

Chapter V

The CCF, 1932-1945

The conference in Calgary in August of 1932 brought together for the first time delegates from most of the major farm and labour groups in the west. Their purpose was the founding of a new political party, but it was not to be a duplicate of the "old line parties," nor was it to be like the Progressive party. The new organization was to be a federation of the existing labour and farm groups; it was also to have a clearly defined political philosophy—socialism. Its purpose was spelled out in the formal resolution passed unanimously by the delegates:

> The establishment in Canada of a co-operative commonwealth in which the basic principle regulating production, distribution, and exchange, will be the supplying of human needs instead of the making of profits.[1]

The name of the new party was to be The Co-operative Commonwealth Federation (Farmer, Labour, Socialist).

The three words included parenthetically at the end of the name indicated that while all the delegates accepted the ideal of the co-operative commonwealth, not all would call themselves socialists; even among those who did, there was some disagreement about what socialism really was. Among the delegates from British Columbia, for example, were those who thought of socialism as the doctrine formulated by Karl Marx. Others had learned their socialism from the writings of members of the British Fabian Society or from other English socialists. And for some socialism was just a general term that meant they were against the government and the existing economic system because it had reduced them to poverty.

Because all shared the same misgivings about the capitalist system and the working of Canadian politics, they were able to forget their doctrinal differences and agree to work together to bring about changes that would improve their lot and that of Canadians in general. In their enthusiasm for change they could unite behind a program, that was more radical than anything ever advocated by the Progressives, one which declared that "social ownership and co-operative production for use is the only sound economic system."[2]

GOALS AND A PROGRAM

The new organization was not simply a political party, it was a political movement as well. The purpose of the CCF as it emerged from the Calgary conference was not just to win the next election, it was to bring about radical changes in the nature of Canadian society. What the members wanted was to replace the profit motive with that of service to the community and to others. It was a noble ideal. As one observer of the Calgary meeting commented, the delegates "oozed idealism to the detriment of practical experience."[3] The purpose of the movement was to win converts to a new way of thinking. Activity in the House of Commons and on the hustings in election campaigns were two ways of doing this, but not the only ones.

During the winter of 1932-33 the members of the new party devoted themselves to the problems of organizing. The provisional executive invited the League for Social Reconstruction to prepare a statement of the party's principles, a Manifesto. This task was performed largely by Frank Underhill, who wrote the first draft of what became the Regina Manifesto at his summer home in June of 1933. It was discussed by other members of the League and then presented to the first convention of the CCF, which met during August, 1933, in Regina.

Some changes were made but the Manifesto that the convention adopted with enthusiastic cheers was essentially as it had been prepared by Underhill and his colleagues. It remained the basic statement of CCF ideology until 1956 and constituted the most specific statement of Canadian socialism.

The aim of the CCF was made very clear in the opening paragraphs of the Manifesto:

> We aim to replace the present capitalist system, with its inherent injustice and inhumanity, by a social order from which the domination and exploitation of one class by another will be eliminated, in which economic planning will supersede unregulated privated enterprise and competition, and in which genuine democratic self-government, based on economic equality will be possible.[4]

The Manifesto proposed the public ownership of all financial machinery—banks, insurance companies, trust companies and the like—as well as public ownership of public utilities and "all other industries and services essential to social planning." Emphasis was laid on the development of co-operatives, and particular attention was given to the problems of the farmers. There were, as well, proposals for medicare, hospital and dental insurance schemes to be run by the state. The Manifesto closed with a ringing declaration:

> No CCF Government will rest content until it has eradicated capitalism and put into operation the full programme of socialized planning which will lead to the establishment in Canada of the Co-operative Commonwealth.

The program of the new party was most assuredly socialist. It was more socialistic than some of its founders had expected or, in a few instances, were prepared to accept. Farm and labour groups had proposed similar measures before but there had never been such a specific and deliberate program as the Regina Manifesto. The guardians of the sacred institutions of Canadian capitalism declared the program preposterous. The Press and opposition politicians saw it as naked communism.

At Regina J. S. Woodsworth was elected National Chairman—in effect the party leader. But he was not a leader in the traditional sense. The CCF was a federation of smaller parties and movements and it was deliberately designed to ensure the fullest participation by all members in making policy and in directing the affairs of the party. One of the chief criticisms western radicals had of the old parties was that they were undemocratic, controlled by a small clique that was dominated by eastern businessmen. No such state of affairs would be allowed to prevail in the CCF. There would be annual conventions, annual elections of officers, and the party platform would be prepared by the delegates at the annual conventions.

REACTION TO THE NEW PARTY

Despite its democratic structure, critics and opponents of the CCF saw it as a totalitarian and alien force. Few of them understood socialism; most of them equated it with communism. Yet the CCF was clearly a direct descendent of the British Labour Party, at least as far as its ideology was concerned. The program of the CCF advocated radical changes in the Canadian economy and attacked the principle of competition and free enterprise. For many observers this was evidence enough that it was a serious threat to "the Canadian way of life." It was ironic that the CCF soon built up an enviable record in defense of individual liberties and parliamentary democracy.

The opponents of the CCF saw a revolutionary force when they looked at the new party. They feared for their property and their privileges. Some members of the CCF found the party philosophy too radical, while others complained that it was not radical enough. Short of having no political philosophy at all, such disagreement was inevitable. So, too, was the opposition of many people in Canada inevitable, for the kinds of change advocated by the CCF were sweeping and bound to arouse serious disagreement.

Because it stood for radical change, because it proposed to reshape sectors of the Canadian economy and reform aspects of Canadian society, the CCF attracted to its ranks people who were deeply concerned about the nature of the Canadian economic and political systems. Many were convinced that future depressions were certain and would remain incurable unless changes were made. The CCF also attracted people whose own situation drove them away from the old parties into the new movement in search of a satisfactory explanation of a poverty that was not of their making. The commitment of all these people to radical change meant that the CCF was able to succeed where an ordinary party could not. It had little money, only a sketchy organization and no political foothold in any legislature, but it had a growing membership of dedicated people prepared to sacrifice their time and what money they had in the cause of reform.

Typical of this kind of dedicated enthusiasm was that shown by M. J. Coldwell. A school principal in Regina when the party was founded, he seldom turned down an invitation to speak about the CCF. This often meant travelling in freezing weather by sleigh to a distant farm. Sympathetic farmers along the way would supply fresh horses, coffee and hot water bottles. In good weather he would hire a plane, leave after school, fly perhaps a hundred miles to speak and then spend the night at a farm. The next morning he would return to start the school day at nine. Money was scarce but farmers would contribute what produce they could spare: a sack of grain here, a bushel of potatoes there.

The CCF stimulated dedication because it offered an explanation of what had gone wrong and proposed what seemed to be a sensible way of preventing the same thing from happening again. In addition, it was a party that clearly belonged to the members. It provided a social focal point, bringing together men and women with similar problems and similar points of view. On the prairie the party meetings were social activities, as were the fund raising efforts—box socials, picnics and the like. In the cities the CCF groups provided a congenial social nucleus for the unemployed, helping many to overcome the feeling that they were Canada's forgotten people. It helped combat the loneliness of the underdog. The character of the CCF as a movement gave it strength and determination far beyond its numbers and financial resources.

THE STRUGGLE FOR POLITICAL SUCCESS

Despite its strengths, however, the CCF did not ride the crest of a wave to political success; it achieved office in only one province, and even there not until 1944. At the beginning there was public suspicion to overcome, as well as the internal divisions and inconsistencies of the movement. The CCF was not a united party; it was a federation of provincial movements and parties, each with a fairly high degree of autonomy of both action and viewpoint. In the three prairie provinces there was a good deal of consistency of philosophy. But British Columbia socialism was more militant and more highly spiced with Marxist or "scientific socialism." Some members in that province had little use for the farmers. The Ontario wing was troubled with discontent resulting from the willingness of some members and some CCF clubs to enter into a alliance with the Communist party. In 1934 Woodsworth had to reorganize the Ontario party to overcome these problems.

The lack of unity was not surprising. Ideology invites dispute, and there were members of the CCF whose main interest was argument rather than political organization. The movement also had a different character in different regions. For example, on the prairie it was growing as part of the rural community. The active leaders of the wheat pools and the co-operative movement were virtually all active in the CCF. On the other hand, in British Columbia, and to a slightly lesser extent in Ontario, the militants were more the "outsiders" of society, the determined non-conformists. Thus, although the CCF was growing, it was growing slowly and not without some internal discomfort.

The national party faced its first serious test in the 1935 federal election. It nominated 119 candidates but only seven were elected: two in Manitoba, two in Saskatchewan and three in British Columbia. This was not an auspicious beginning. The Ginger Group had been wiped out and there were no CCF members at all from Alberta. In that province an even newer political phenomenon, Social Credit, had swept all before it. In all, the CCF got only 9 percent of the total popular vote and only 2 percent of the seats in the House of Commons.

The election of 1935 was a confusing one for the voter. In many constituencies there were five and occasionally six candidates. A former Conservative cabinet minister, H. H. Stevens, had created a new party, the Reconstruction party. It ran 174 candidates but elected only one. Nevertheless, it attracted close to 400,000 votes. Social Credit, in winning every seat in Alberta, cut heavily into support that might otherwise have gone to the CCF. It is likely that some of those who voted Reconstruction and Social Credit would have voted CCF, although it is impossible to say how many. However it was explained, though, the result of the election was a blow to the CCF.

The party fought a vigorous and direct campaign. Party

literature pulled no punches; if anything, it was a bit too sharp in its criticism of capitalism. One CCF pamphlet read:

Bank Robbers Get Millions, but the BIG SHOT BANKER IS A BIGGER CRIMINAL THAN THE GUNMAN because the banker's greed hurts all the people all the time.[5]

Another urged voters to "Smash the Big Shots' Slave Camps and Sweat Shops."[6] From the CCF point of view capitalism had caused the depression; but this was not quite the same thing as accusing bankers of criminal greed. For the active members of the CCF the enemy was plain to see—the men who controlled the financial structure of Canada, those who suffered little during the depression. Rid the economy of their unwholesome influence, place the public in control, and the problem would be solved. There was some truth in their analysis, and their vehemence was understandable, but it did not attract many voters who were not already socialists. Indeed, it repelled many.

With only six members in a House of Commons composed of 254, the CCF seemed to be of little consequence when the new parliament opened. But as session followed session it became clear that Woodsworth and his colleagues were the real opposition to Mackenzie King's Liberal administration. After the departure of R. B. Bennett, the Conservatives groped for leadership and policy; they were to stumble in the darkness of opposition for twenty-two years. The CCF, however, did have a leader of considerable ability and a clearly defined policy. The members of the small group were dedicated to their cause and managed to do the work of a caucus at least thrice their size. In the first session, for example, T. C. Douglas spoke sixty times, more than most members and as much as most cabinet ministers.

The role the CCF played was that of the conscience of the House of Commons, speaking out on behalf of those whose interests seemed to be ignored by the government, and championing the cause of civil rights. In the latter cause the small band was able to bring about the repeal of section 98 of the Criminal Code, the infamous section that had first made its appearance during the Winnipeg general strike in 1919, permitting the arrest and deportation of "aliens." In 1937 the CCF led a concerted attack on the inroads being made into civil liberties by provincial governments, notably those of Premier Mitchell Hepburn of Ontario and Premier Duplessis of Quebec. In both cases the police power of the state was being used to interfere with the legitimate activities of trade unions in strikes and union organization. In particular, the CCF attack was directed against the Padlock Law in Quebec, a law that enabled the arbitrary arrest of individuals who, contrary to established procedure, were then required to prove their innocence. While the CCF could not change these laws, by bringing them to the attention of the nation through debate in the House of Commons they were able to arouse public opinion and, on occasion, force the government to act.

In 1939 Woodsworth had the satisfaction of seeing the government introduce legislation guaranteeing the right of employees to form and join trade unions. He had been advocating such a bill for three years. By standing firmly on principle, by

The CCF caucus, 1937: left to right, Tommy Douglas, Angus Mac-Innis, A. A. Heaps, J. S. Woodsworth, M. J. Coldwell, Grace MacInnis and Grant MacNeil. Coldwell succeeded Woodsworth as party leader. Douglas became first leader of the NDP. Mrs. MacInnis, Woodsworth's daughter, was active in both the CCF and NDP.

raising issues again and again and by patient and carefully prepared argument, the CCF members were able to induce the government to introduce reforms that would otherwise have been much longer in coming. Their very presence in the House of Commons was a constant reminder to the Liberal government of the sizeable body of the electorate that were in favour of broad and far-reaching reform. Political commentators may not have supported the CCF philosophy, but they were forced to admit time and again that the six CCF MP's were an efficient and formidable opposition to the government.

During this early period the members of the CCF were active across the country, bringing in new members, organizing clubs and constituency associations and eagerly looking toward the day when a CCF government would be in power. In Saskatchewan in 1934 the Farmer-Labour party had become the official opposition in the provincial legislature winning five seats—the Liberal government held the other fifty. In 1938 the CCF increased this standing to ten seats. In British Columbia the CCF became the official opposition in 1941, winning more votes than any other party. Membership in the party grew, but not as quickly as party leaders had hoped. Despite its British ancestry, Canadian socialism remained a strange and, for many, a sinful doctrine. The fact that opponents of the CCF constantly referred to it as a communist "front" did not help. Nor did the repeated public invitations of the Communist party to join forces help the CCF image.

THE CCF DURING THE WAR

The outbreak of war in 1939 found the CCF stronger than it had been in 1933, but not as strong as its founders had expected. The war brought a more prosperous economy. The production of war materials took up the slack in industry, the prices of farm produce improved, and the army offered employment for many who had spent the previous three or four years on relief. The war also brought a crisis in the CCF.

As a man of deep religious faith and strict adherence to principle, Woodsworth had opposed war all his life. For him the organized slaughter of one's fellow men, regardless of the cause, was not an acceptable policy. He could not support Canada's entry into the war. A majority of his fellow party members, however, did not take this position. Most were opposed to war in principle, but at the same time they accepted the fact of Hitler's ambitions in Europe and the unfortunate necessity of resisting him with force. From the day of its foundation the CCF had officially opposed war. The crisis of 1939 brought about an agonizing reappraisal of that policy.

At a long and emotionally charged meeting of the party's National Council, it was decided that Woodsworth would stand alone, stating his opposition to the war while M. J. Coldwell would speak for the party and support Canada's entry at Britain's side. In his speech to parliament Woodsworth said:

> I have every respect for the man who, with a sincere conviction, goes out to give his life if necessary in a cause which he believes to be right; but I have just as much respect for the man who refuses to enlist to kill his fellow men and, as under modern conditions, to kill women and children as well . . . .[7]

The point was, he insisted, that "brute force" was being allowed to overcome "moral force."

During the debate Prime Minister Mackenzie King said:

> There are few men in this parliament for whom, in some particulars, I have greater respect than the leader of the Co-operative Commonwealth Federation. I admire him in my heart because time and again he has had the courage to say what lay on his conscience regardless of what the world might think of him. A man of that calibre is an ornament to any Parliament . . . .[8]

It was a fitting tribute to Woodsworth at a time when, his health failing and the party he had led opposing him, he stood firmly on those principles that his intellect and his conscience had told him were right and just.

The CCF entered the wartime parliament after the 1940 election with eight seats, only two more than before; but this time five were from Saskatchewan. They had lost one seat in Manitoba and two in British Columbia. There had been little change in the popular vote received. There was one ray of hope—the party had an MP from Nova Scotia, Clarence Gillis. His election was a direct result of the affiliation with the party, in 1938, of the Cape Breton local of the United Mine Workers Union. From 1936 on the party had made a determined effort to interest trade unions in providing support. The case they made was a good one: the CCF was the only party in the House of Commons that supported all the demands of organized labour. The election of Gillis was the first dividend from that policy.

The role of opposition in wartime is awkward and difficult. The government of the day tends to seek refuge in the cloak of patriotism or the spurious caves of secrecy. The CCF entered the war uneasily, with an ailing and alienated leader and little hope of improving its political position. As it turned out, during the period 1940-1945 the CCF was to reach the highwater mark in its fortunes.

*　　*　　*

The period of "the dirty thirties" passed and war, relief measures, and the gradual institution of Keynesian* economic policies pulled the country out of the chasm of the depression. Despite dire predictions, there had been no revolution, socialism had not swept the land, and the thousands of unemployed and economically deprived did not rise up and overthrow established authority. But in western Canada notice had been clearly given that the politics of the traditional parties had been weighed, found wanting and rejected. The spectre of a socialist take-over remained to haunt the leaders of the Liberal and Conservative parties. Many people were also surprised by the remarkable surge to power of the Social Credit party—which was something quite different again.

The depression had demonstrated with tragic clarity the need for direct government intervention in the economy on a permanent basis. There would be no returning to the "good old days" of the free economy. The depression had also demonstrated the efficacy of government activity, something which the war further empha-

---

*John Maynard Keynes (1883-1946) was a British economist whose theories challenged the orthodox views of the day and had profound significance throughout the western world. One of his major works, *The General Theory of Employment, Interest and Money* (1936), attacked traditional fatalism in regard to mass unemployment. Keynes argued that public (government) spending should be timed for maximum effect. At the onset of recession, he suggested, government expenditure should be increased so as to increase employment and thus through the payment of wages, raise spending power and stimulate business investment.

sised. It was during the depression—and under the aegis of a Conservative government—that the CBC, the Bank of Canada and the basis for Trans Canada Airlines had been established. As prosperity returned to those who had known the despair of poverty, it brought with it a determination to ensure that poverty would never return. Thus it was, ironically, that the CCF did not ride to great prominence and to power in Saskatchewan in the trough of despondency, but on the crest of rising expectations that grew during the war.

Chapter VI

The CCF: Left, Right and Centre

By 1940 J. S. Woodsworth was leader of the national CCF in name only. His health was failing and his appearances in parliament became infrequent. At the national convention of the party that year he was, in effect, retired. The office of National President was abolished and Woodsworth was made Honorary President. M. J. Coldwell was made National Chairman. When Woodsworth died two years later, Coldwell became party leader.

Although he was party leader, M. J. Coldwell had less freedom of action in party affairs than did his opposite numbers in the Liberal and Conservative parties. They had more independence and were only indirectly responsible to their parties or to the key figures in their parties. Coldwell was elected leader for only two years at a time. He had to maintain close contact and consultation with the party and its elected officials on the CCF executive and National Council. At each biennial convention he was expected to give an account of his stewardship to the delegates. The CCF not only believed in democracy, but practised it in party affairs as much as the demands of political combat permitted.

THE GROWTH OF INFLUENCE

Coldwell found himself at the head of a party that was, contrary to popular expectation, increasing in both size and influence. Its growth in size was due in some measure to the unsettling effects of the war. The dislocation caused through enlistment in the armed forces, by changes in living habits necessitated by rationing, by new work patterns, and the effect of wartime propaganda, made people "future-oriented." That is to say, they looked forward to peacetime. The CCF was unique in that its program laid great stress on preparing for the postwar period.

There was apprehension that the end of the war might herald the return of hard times. Here again the CCF seemed to be the one party with some answers.

Professor Lipset, in his study of the CCF in Saskatchewan has commented on the "phenomenon of intensified radical behavior in a period of prosperity following a depression." The depression had caused a great deal of political apathy, particularly among the farmers, who had been the poorest:

> Those who are on the bottom of the economic scale will not revolt if they are pushed down farther. A person must have a certain amount of security to fight for a larger share.

When the war and social legislation brought an improvement in the condition of the farmer and the worker, they began to consider ways of securing their position.

Professor Lipset points out:

> The return of prosperity removes the main cause of political apathy among the poorer farmers and workers. The radical movement is able to capitalize on the adverse experiences of the poorer classes during the depression. The CCF in Canada was able to convince many workers and farmers that a change in the economic system would prevent a new depression. The resentment of the lower strata of the population over their treatment during the depression was therefore channeled during prosperity.[1]

As the influence of the CCF grew, the government of Mackenzie King became aware of this new rival. Fearful of losing seats, King sought to head off the CCF by moving to the left and adopting some of the less radical CCF proposals. Throughout the war Mackenzie King referred frequently in his diary to the CCF. Always he indicated his mounting concern that the new party would overtake and unseat his Liberal government. Whenever he proposed welfare measures to his cabinet, he justified them by mentioning the CCF threat. In 1943, referring to a speech he had made, King wrote:

> Dealt strong blow for the living standard of the masses of the people from coast to coast. I think I have cut out the ground in large part from under the CCF and Tories alike . . . .[2]

A year later, defending his government's air transport policy against the demands of the CPR for more private air routes, King wrote:

> . . . had our Government not taken the position we did, we would simply have been leaving the way open for the CCF to take it as their policy . . . .[3]

It required little skill to see that the CCF was developing sinews it had not had in the thirties. In February, 1942, an unknown CCF'er, Joseph Noseworthy, defeated the leader of the Conservative party, Arthur Meighen, in a by-election. Of eight by-elections it contested during the early forties, the CCF won four. The Gallup Poll indicated that CCF popular support across the country had leaped from 9 percent in 1940 to 29 percent in 1943. In September, 1943, more people said they would vote CCF than for either the Liberal or Conservative parties. That same year the Ontario CCF won thirty-nine of ninety seats in the provincial election. A year later the first socialist government in North America was formed in Saskatchewan when the CCF won forty-seven of the fifty-two seats in the provincial legislature.

TOWARD A RECONCILIATION OF FARM AND LABOUR

Socialists throughout Canada were encouraged by these two provincial successes. They seemed to prove that socialism was finally on the march to national success. What the two happy events really showed was that CCF strength lay in two different directions, directions that, if not opposites, were clearly not parallel. In Ontario the party was urban; it drew much of its support from the working and lower middle class strata in the cities. The Ontario party relied heavily on trade union support, and its activities were more akin to those of the older parties. In Saskatchewan, on the other hand, the strength of the party was obviously among the farmers who had come up through the tradition of the United Farmers and the Progressives. There was little trade union involvement in Saskatchewan—there were too few trade unions. And in that province the orientation of the party was more middle class. Its organization depended to a great extent on party activity providing the social and recreational focus in farm communities.

Unlike the factory worker, the farmer was not an employee; he was often an employer and always a producer. He was a kind of capitalist; he owned some, or all of his farm, and he had a considerable investment in heavy equipment and machinery. He had helped build the protest movements of the twenties and thirties because his expectations had not been met and his pleas for aid had been ignored. He did not support the capitalist system as it was then working. The socialism of the CCF appealed to him, for it meant that he could exercise control over government-owned enterprise through his MLA or MP, whereas he had no influence over the private businesses that had treated him so badly when the price of wheat was low or when his crops had failed.

It is worth noting that the farmer did not favour public ownership of land. The single family farm was an article of faith. Furthermore, the Saskatchewan farmer did not oppose profits, especially those he made in selling his produce. Significantly, the Saskatchewan wing of the CCF omitted from its provincial program any statement that opposed the making of profits.

On the other hand, the farmer supported welfare measures because they made sense and did not interfere with his freedom to make a good living on the farm. In general, though, he supported the CCF because it was the party he had helped create, which listened to him and gave him every opportunity to participate in its policy decisions.

Outside Saskatchewan the strength the CCF developed during the war evaporated almost as quickly as it had formed. In the 1945 Ontario election, the party's vote did not fall too drastically, but it lost all but seven of the seats it had won in 1943. The federal election that followed was less disappointing, but the surge to power that many in the CCF felt was in the offing failed to materialize. The popular vote doubled and twenty-eight MPs were elected; this was still a long way from forming a government.

The CCF fought the 1945 federal election on basically the same program it had used in 1940. Party speeches and pamphlets warned the electorate that the return to peacetime practices would bring another depression unless more socialistic measures were adopted. Some people were won over in this way, but many stayed with the old parties. Their refusal to change

The Medicine Man

Said a medicine salesman named Coldwell:
"My Story sounds good when it's told well,
I have wonderful cures
And Glittering lures
But, Doggone it, the stuff hasn't sold well."

Said Lewis, "You can't hope to sell
A bottle with such taste and smell,
But wrap it in fable,
Keep changing the label,
Then the contents nobody can tell."

"With my line of sales talk," said Winch,
"To market this snake oil's a cinch.
It's a tepid solution
Of pink revolution,
And those who won't drink it we'll pinch."

"This potent elixir," said Knowles,
"Is good for their bodies and souls.
It makes 'em all dizzy
And dreamy and fizzy,
And softens 'em up for the polls."

A cartoon from the *Winnipeg Free Press*, June 8, 1945. The chief characters are Ernest Winch, David Lewis, and Stanley Knowles, pioneers in the CCF, and M. J. Coldwell, the leader of the party.

had been reinforced by a massive anti-CCF propaganda campaign financed by several of the major banks and businesses in Canada. These firms were led by men who agreed completely with Arthur Meighen, the patrician spokesman of the Canadian right wing, when he said in 1943:

> The CCF is a menace to this country and will be the "left" party of the future. It has all the fakes and fanatics now within its compass and their number is legion . . . .[4]

Beginning shortly after the CCF successes in Ontario and Saskatchewan, pamphlets attacking the CCF were mailed to every household in the country. Employers put notes in their employees' pay-envelopes urging them not to vote for the socialist party. How much responsibility for the failure of the CCF can be traced to these campaigns is difficult to say. On the assumption that advertising has some effect, the pamphlets and newspaper advertisements must have done considerable damage.

While the party was reaping the harvest of patient and tireless activity in Saskatchewan, efforts were being made to bring the trade unions in Canada into closer association with the party. As pointed out earlier, there was a great deal that the unions and the CCF had in common, apart from the fact that several labour parties and trade union councils had played a part in founding the CCF. Woodsworth had been instrumental in winning for labour the legal right to organize; Stanley Knowles, one of the ablest CCF MP's, had fought a long campaign to protect the pension rights of workers; and, at the national level, the party had devoted as much time to the problems of labour as it had to the needs of the farmer.

In some respects the CCF had won the battle for the farmer: after the war there was no repetition of the hard times that were the common lot of the wheat producer before 1940. But trade unions were still only barely tolerated. In Ontario and Quebec harsh and repressive measures had been used either to limit the activities of unions before the war, or to destroy them altogether. The employer was still king.

Recognizing their common interests, the Canadian Congress of Labour, which represented most of the industrial unions in Canada, endorsed the CCF in 1943 as the "political arm of labour."[5] By this act the CCL provided the basis for more formal co-operation between the two groups. (In fact, there had been a great deal of informal contact between the trade union movement and the CCF before this time.) In the period following the end of the war, the trade union movement became a major source of party funds and personnel. Unlike the Liberal and Conservative parties, which received their funds from corporations and individual donations, until the late forties the CCF was financed almost entirely by membership dues. After the forties, a number of trade unions made lump-sum contributions or assisted by paying the salaries of party organizers.

The decade that followed the war was one in which the CCF managed to hold its own, although it did not advance. In Saskatchewan several of the government's ventures into public ownership had failed and these failures were trumpeted across the land by a universally hostile press. Of the successes less was heard, but they included government operated automobile insurance, provincially run transportation and ambulance services, and the first hospital insurance scheme in Canada. The willingness of Premier T. C. Douglas' administration to adopt new schemes and examine new ideas attracted a number of bright young men into the province's civil service. Despite the stigma of its socialism, the Saskatchewan administration was considered a model in several respects and was frequently visited by members of other governments seeking advice and anxious to learn from the Saskatchewan experience.

RE-EXAMINATION AND RENEWAL

By 1950 it had become obvious to the national leaders of the CCF that the Regina Manifesto had become dated. Socialist parties throughout the free world had been revising their programs, and in some cases their basic beliefs, in the light of changing conditions and the experience of socialist governments. In Canada, the strength of the CCF was now clearly more urban than rural. Ontario provided more CCF votes than Saskatchewan; British Columbia, where the party was again an urban movement, was a close third. The party executive believed that a new program would bring the CCF up to date, free it of the old "days of the depression" outlook that was no longer relevant.

The Canadian economy had experienced some slumps since the war and unemployment had been severe at times, but conditions were nothing like those of the thirties. Partly because of the constant goading of the CCF and their fear that it might overtake them, the Liberals had introduced a series of welfare measures that made unemployment and economic slumps easier for the public to bear. Canada had achieved a level of prosperity that made the angry criticism of the thirties out of date.

In its official statements the CCF no longer opposed small scale business. Instead, its attacks were directed against monopolies and large corporate enterprises which, the party argued, exercised power without responsibility. The program advanced by the CCF, it was said, should be designed to help employer and employee alike. The CCF leaders felt this modification of the party program was not only consistent with the changing temper of democratic socialism throughout the world, it was also consistent with the gradual movement together of the trade unions and the CCF. Most of the leaders of the major industrial unions in Canada were committed socialists and, although the same was not yet true of rank and file unionists, the national CCF grew more dependent on trade union support. Consequently its policies tended to reflect attitudes more consistent with the less radical ideology of the trade union movement.

Between 1950 and 1956 the party worked on various drafts of a new program. In 1956 a new statement of principles was adopted by the national convention meeting in Winnipeg. This statement became known as the Winnipeg Declaration. A much shorter document than the Regina Manifesto, the Declaration had the same moral tone: co-operation is better than competition, capitalism is "basically immoral." [6] But the specific proposals were more consistent with the modern welfare state and proposed little public ownership beyond public utilities. The emphasis was on reform and improving the quality of life through such things as better education and health services.

The new look in Canadian socialism did little to improve the party's fortunes. The year after the publication of the Declaration, in the election that swept the Liberals out of office after twenty-two years in power, the CCF improved its vote only slightly and found itself with but 25 of the 265 seats in the House of Commons. A year later, when John Diefenbaker and the

Conservatives swept into office with the largest majority in Canadian history, the party was decimated. Only eight CCF MP's remained, and these did not include the party leader, M. J. Coldwell, or such party stalwarts as Stanley Knowles and Colin Cameron.

In 1955 the two labour congresses in Canada, the Canadian Congress of Labour and the Trades and Labour Congress had joined forces to become the Canadian Labour Congress. Although it did not specifically endorse the CCF as the political arm of labour, the new Congress was clearly more sympathetic toward the CCF than any other party. In April of 1958 the CLC adopted a proposal to co-operate with the CCF in the creation of a new political party. In July of that year the CCF national convention adopted a similar motion. For the next three years, under the direction of a joint committee, the two groups engaged in the process of forming a new base for the Canadian left.

The "New Party," as it was then called, was to include three groups: the labour people, CCF members and people who were classified as "liberally minded"—meaning those who were in neither of the other groups but in general sympathy with their aims. The committee organized seminars across the country and set up "New Party clubs" to discuss the proposed program. The process was remarkable in that it constituted the first example of nation-wide, grass-roots participation in the creation of a new political party.

Not all members of the CCF welcomed the new adventure with enthusiasm. For some it was a confirmation of their suspicions that socialism would disappear with the CCF and that the new party would be more like the Liberal and Conservative parties—more anxious for office than reform. In British Columbia the provincial executive refused to endorse the formation of New Party clubs; the same was true in Alberta; and there was little apparent enthusiasm in Saskatchewan or Manitoba.

Despite the reticence of many in the CCF, the new party was formally created in Ottawa in July, 1961. It was called the New Democratic Party, or NDP. T. C. Douglas was elected leader, and subsequently resigned as Premier of Saskatchewan. The NDP faced its first federal election in 1962. In every province but Saskatchewan its vote was greater than that of the CCF in 1958, but not by more than 5½ percent.

The new party that the CCF had helped create was more like a labour party in the British tradition than the CCF had been. It was still interested in the farmer's vote and in his problems, but these were relatively insignificant alongside the potential support of the people in the cities who were now much worse off than the farmers.

AN ASSESSMENT

The Co-operative Commonwealth Federation closed the book on nearly thirty years of vigorous and conscientious effort in the field of political, social and economic reform. Its notable political success was the government of Saskatchewan, but there were other successes, less notable because they were evident only to those who followed closely the business of politics and parliament in Canada. Scholars are agreed that many reforms introduced by Mackenzie King came when they did because he feared growing CCF popularity. Political commentators were unanimous in singling out CCF members of parliament for their persistent and skilful defense of civil liberties and their effectiveness as government critics. Members of the party could draw satisfaction from the existence of laws that provided for the orderly marketing of grain through a government board, national hospital insurance, family allowances, old age pensions, medicare and many other measures—all enacted by other parties in power, but first advocated by the CCF.

Politicians, as a rule, derive cold comfort from seeing their pet policies adopted by other parties, but the members of the CCF as participants in a movement did find satisfaction in this situation. Their movement had certain goals and if these were achieved, even by the Liberals, then the movement had been a success in that respect. The obvious failure of the CCF *party* to win power did not affect the partial success of the CCF *movement*. By 1961 the welfare state in Canada was well on its way with further advances on the horizon, such as national health insurance—a measure pioneered in North America by the Saskatchewan CCF.

The record of the CCF was not a bad one. Federally, however, the party had never managed to win more than 15 percent of the popular vote at any time in its history. It failed in this respect because of several factors, not the least significant of which was the predominance of capitalist attitudes in Canada. People equated democracy with free enterprise and, conversely, socialism with communism. In this view they were, for obvious reasons, supported by the economic élite. Like the trade unions, the CCF was seen as a sinister force in Canadian politics, and this attitude was reinforced by virtually every newspaper in Canada. The CCF had to break down barriers of prejudice that were constantly being shored up by its opponents. It never had enough money to campaign effectively and often what money it did have was wasted on wordy and ill-designed literature that was seldom read. The party was also often hampered by the excessive zeal of its own members who said things that provided opponents with the opportunity to label the party as subversive.

Nevertheless, by its very existence the CCF offered a continuing reminder of the importance of principle and the necessity of dissent in a democracy. At a time when conformity was becoming almost a continental characteristic, the CCF demonstrated the importance of honest and forthright opposition to the *status quo*. It was not an easy role to play, yet thousands of Canadians through active participation in the affairs of the party showed a willingness to stand as outsiders because of their beliefs. The emphasis on membership and active participation in politics that typified the CCF gradually became a standard in Canadian politics. The Liberal and Conservative parties began to move toward greater democracy in their internal structures and operations following the example set by the socialist party.

*   *   *

Almost all the members of the CCF continued to work in the NDP. In fact, at the executive level there were no visible changes. The goal was essentially that of the CCF, although it was seen as perhaps more remote: the establishment of the co-operative commonwealth in Canada. The new party was moving more slowly in that direction, paying more attention to the niceties of public relations and refurbishing or discarding old doctrine with almost callous indifference to the memory of those who had first fashioned the instrument of reform in Regina in 1933.

Chapter VII

The Coming of Social Credit

In Alberta there was no provincial CCF. The United Farmers of Alberta affiliated with the CCF in 1932 and, therefore, represented that party in the provincial field. When the United Farmers were defeated in 1935 they pulled the CCF down with them, never to rise again in that province. Thus there occurred the curious phenomenon of two provinces, side by side, sharing economic, geographic and, to some extent, cultural characteristics, but with governments that espoused political views at almost opposite ends of the ideological spectrum. By 1944 there was a socialist government in Saskatchewan and a Social Credit government in Alberta. And Social Credit had been in power since 1935.

In 1921, the year of the sudden rise of the Progressives, the United Farmers of Alberta became the government of Alberta. They stayed in office with roughly two-thirds of the seats until 1935—through two more elections. The government formed by the farmers' party was more radical than the Liberal administration it replaced, but a lot more conservative than the UFA had originally set out to be. The element of delegate democracy appeared as a faint shadow of the original doctrine, and group government did not appear at all. The elected Members of the Legislature chose their leader, but he had a free hand in choosing the cabinet. Apart from fairly effective influence exerted on the government by the annual UFA convention, there was little change in the processes of government after 1921. As a result, many farmers became disenchanted with the orthodoxy of the UFA administration under both Premier Greenfield and his successor, Premier Brownlee. The cabinet seemed to be as much in control as before.

The theories of social credit were not known in Alberta, or

the rest of Canada for that matter, before the UFA came to power. Indeed, members of the United Farmers, notably William Irvine, played a vital role in popularizing social credit doctrines. There was, however, no social credit movement in Canada until 1932 when William Aberhart began to introduce political doctrine into his Sunday afternoon religious broadcasts.

THE THEORIES OF MAJOR DOUGLAS

Social credit doctrine originated with Major C. H. Douglas, a Scottish professional engineer. As an engineer, Douglas was thoroughly exasperated with the inefficiency of the capitalist system. There was, he believed, too much waste and under-utilization of resources. One of the problems, he pointed out, was the insufficiency of purchasing power in the economy to fully utilize productive capacity. People did not have enough money to buy all the things that could be made by industry. He advocated that the government distribute money to restore the balance.

To illustrate his point, Douglas propounded the "A plus B Theorem," in which "A" represented the wages paid to employees and "B" the overhead costs of production. To make a pair of shoes, for example, one had to provide leather and machinery —the "B" in the theorem—and pay the wages of the people who did the work—the "A". The price of the shoes, therefore, would have to be "A plus B." But since the employees would only get "A," they would be unable to buy the shoes. To make up the difference, Douglas said, money would have to be created and distributed to consumers as social credit dividends. Social Credit, Douglas said, was essentially a belief in the capacity of the community to deliver the goods and services.[1] The theorem was so deliciously simple that it made sense to everyone, particularly those without enough money to buy the goods which the stores had in quantity; everyone, that is, except economists.

Economists rejected Douglas' theory simply because it did not fit the facts. They had some difficulty, however, demonstrating the fallacy of the theorem. Douglas had been so vague about the assumptions on which it was based that any criticism necessarily involved a rather tedious definition of terms that left most listeners in a state of refined boredom. On one level it could be pointed out that the employees of a shoe factory would not wish, as a body, to buy all the output, so the question does not arise of their not being able to afford to do so. It seems equally true that since there are other firms making other goods their employees will help buy up the shoes produced. It is also obvious that the "B" costs paid for leather and machinery find their way, through wages and dividends, to consumers, some of whom will want a pair of shoes. Economists also pointed out that the creation of additional money to "redress the balance" would merely inflate the economy causing costs and prices to rise. Despite these arguments, the theorem seemed sensible to many people and appeared to fit the facts of the depression. Demonstrations of its inconsistencies were ignored. People under stress believe what they want to believe and reject attempts to convince them otherwise.

The more general aspects of social credit theory as developed and advanced by Major Douglas consisted of an ironclad defense of private ownership and management, and a condemnation of finance and financiers—supposedly the real villains of the economy. The financiers, said Douglas, controlled the entire productive system and manipulated it for their own benefit. They were holding back the realization of the full technological potential of industry to protect their own interests. These same financiers controlled the government. One commentator concludes:

> To the convinced social crediter there were no economic problems left: the Douglas theory provided solutions for them all and the necessary technical devices could easily be worked out by experts.[2]

The real problem was getting political power in order to introduce social credit.

The political theory of social credit was not group government, as advocated earlier by the leaders of the United Farmers; it was government by experts. Douglas could see no point in convening a parliament of men with no special skills for governing, and then expecting them to make detailed laws for specific problems. He argued that the function of the elected member is to provide the general goals for society, while the experts in the civil service make the specific plans and are provided the means and power for implementing them. Douglas might have con-

assisted with unflinching loyalty by a young graduate of the Institute, Ernest C. Manning.

The depression hit Alberta hard. It was disastrous for the farmer. It was also disastrous for many in the cities. In Calgary the sudden collapse of the oil boom, which had earlier lured people into stock speculation, wiped out many small fortunes and many more nest eggs. Destitution and despair were the common coin of the province. Brownlee's UFA government wrestled with the problem, but had nothing to offer except traditional conservative policies. The depression also caused a drop in attendance at Aberhart's Bible Institute and a diminution in donations. Aberhart was distressed. This distress was increased when a student in Crescent Heights school committed suicide as a direct result of his parents' sudden poverty.

In the summer of 1932 Aberhart was introduced to the doctrines of Major Douglas for the first time. His conversion was rapid. Before long the Bible Institute became a centre of social credit teaching and propaganda; the Sunday broadcasts wove the doctrines of social credit into the fabric of religious fundamentalism. For Aberhart social credit was the answer. For his listeners and followers it became a godsend because, like fundamentalism, if offered a simple, unsophisticated analysis and a pat answer to the problems that pressed upon them.

Throughout that winter and the following year, Aberhart and Manning formed study groups in Calgary, spoke to meetings and circulated pamphlets. Aberhart threw his abilities as an orator into the campaign. His speeches on social credit "were interlaced with much emotional rhetoric about the impact of the depression on the people of Alberta, coupled with impassioned moral and religious exhortations and frequent references to Bible prophecy."[5] Meetings were also held outside the province as interest in social credit grew through the influence of the Sunday afternoon broadcasts. During the summer of 1933 Aberhart and Manning were almost constantly on tour throughout Alberta. They had meetings before overflow crowds of farmers, many of whom came forty or fifty miles to attend.

Aberhart was not an expert on social credit. By 1934 the doctrinaire social crediters were increasingly critical of the free interpretation he gave to their doctrines. The criticism reached its peak in 1934 when the Douglas Secretariat in London, England, wrote to Aberhart informing him that they could not endorse his movement and asking him to remove the name "Douglas" from his pamphlet, *The Douglas System of Economics.* Unless he preached the true doctrine, they said, Aberhart was not entitled to use the name of the founder.

Aberhart called a mass meeting in Calgary and announced that it would be his last address on the Douglas system. Before a crowded and emotionally charged audience he said he was being persecuted for wrongs he had not committed. Wrapping himself in the mantle of the martyr, he announced that he would resign as president of the Social Credit movement. He did not tell his listeners that his particular version of social credit differed from that of its originator, Major C. H. Douglas.

Shortly after this event, Major Douglas himself came to Alberta at the invitation of the UFA government. He agreed to speak at a public meeting in Calgary. At the same time he declined Aberhart's invitation to speak on the Sunday afternoon broadcast from the Bible Institute. When the public meeting was held, Aberhart was on the platform but, despite the cries of, "We want Aberhart!" from the audience, he did not speak. Douglas did, for two hours. The meeting ended in discord when it became clear that Aberhart would not be invited to speak. Douglas never addressed another meeting in Alberta. His speech, while obviously the true doctrine, was irrelevant where Alberta was concerned because he did not understand the situation in the province. To the people of the province it was crystal clear that Aberhart had the answers. By the beginning of June, 1934, Aberhart was back at the helm of the Social Credit movement.

The Social Credit movement had developed basically as an educational campaign with no political overtones. Aberhart was not, in those early days, bent on becoming head of the Alberta government, although there must have been times when this prospect flitted across his mind. Until 1934 Aberhart and his followers were preaching the salvation of Alberta through the adoption by the government of their version of social credit principles. The doctrine had a magic appeal to people stricken by the depression, and Aberhart's following across the province grew.

The fact that orthodox business leaders and economists opposed the ideas Aberhart expounded only lent extra force to his crusade. One of the cornerstones of social credit was condemnation of the business and financial interests who, it was claimed, were responsible for the perversion of the free enterprise system that produced depressions. The farmers, it was said, could expect nothing better from such men.

When the Alberta legislature held hearings to investigate the validity of Douglas' social credit doctrine, both Douglas and Aberhart appeared. Douglas was vague and ambiguous. He stressed the problems of implementing his program in Alberta in the light of the limitations imposed by the Canadian constitution. Aberhart was direct and positive:

> Given the power, either I or dozens of other people could provide you in three months with a scheme which would work perfectly and put Alberta, or Canada . . . forever outside the range of poverty.[6]

The government of Alberta was not impressed with the arguments of either Aberhart or Douglas, although the latter had impressed them as more cautious and conscious of the problems. They decided to do nothing to implement either the Douglasite or Aberhart schemes. This distressed the citizens of the province who had become convinced that Aberhart could save Alberta.

POLITICAL POWER ACHIEVED

When Premier John Brownlee had to resign after unsuccessfully defending himself in a paternity suit, there was a growing feeling that only one man and one movement could alleviate the effects of the depression. By midsummer of 1934 Aberhart was moving inexorably toward the establishment of his movement as a political party. In December he announced that at the next provincial election "reliable, honourable, bribe-proof businessmen who have definitely laid aside their party politic affiliations, will be asked to represent Social Credit in every constituency."[7] A month later the UFA convention refused to adopt social credit theories, and with that the Social Credit movement became a political party, bent on winning the next election.

The campaign was unique in Canadian history. The Social Credit party had a head start on the others. While Aberhart travelled across the prairie in the summer of 1934, insisting that Social Credit was an educational movement, his followers were organizing the movement in constituency groups. In the autumn mid-week radio broadcasts were begun, featuring short plays written by Aberhart and Manning. The central character of these dramas was the "Man from Mars," a creature who could not understand why the people of Alberta had not already instituted social credit.

During the campaign Aberhart reduced social credit to a few slogans that were low in intellectual content but high on emotional content. He promised his listeners that a Social Credit government would institute a system of dividends whereby everyone in the province would receive a monthly payment of twenty-five dollars. When people insisted that they did not know how the scheme was going to work, he pointed out:

> You don't have to know all about Social Credit before you vote for it; you don't have to understand electricity to use it . . . all you have to do is push the button and you get the light.[8]

The experts would take care of all the details. Social Credit, he claimed, was going to bring to an end the poverty in the midst of plenty that plagued Albertans.

The Social Credit campaign was tightly controlled from Calgary headquarters at the Bible Institute. All the candidates were personally selected by Aberhart, and he constantly urged his followers to stand together and trust the leaders of the movement. Under such careful control and driven by the force of his personality, Aberhart's Social Credit movement swept across Alberta like a brush fire. In January, 1935, the movement held a straw poll in every constituency to determine how much support they had. The result showed that 93 percent of those responding favoured Social Credit. Despite the nature of the organization, those who supported it did so believing it to be not a party but a movement that was above and beyond politics. For many of these people it took on the character of a crusade.

The enthusiasm of most Albertans for Social Credit created great difficulties for politicians of the other parties. Ex-premier

Brownlee spoke to a meeting in Waterglen that seemed quiet and successful until he began to discuss Social Credit:

> So I began to tell them in all sincerity what I thought of Social Credit. A group of big fellows near the door then left the hall, slamming the door violently as they went out. Some of them then got into cars and started to blow horns. Others got logs and began pounding the walls and doors of the building from outside, while they hooted and yelled. Some of my supporters went outside and the rough stuff stopped. But the meeting inside was in a tumultuous uproar.[9]

Other UFA leaders had the same experience, as one reported:

> ... just as soon as it became apparent that I was going to discuss Aberhart's theories in a critical way, down went the people's heads. The men would scowl fiercely at me. They didn't want to hear Aberhart criticized. If the Apostle Paul had been loose in Alberta for six months, he couldn't have stopped Social Credit.[10]

There was very little the opposition to Aberhart could do. The mayor of Vancouver, Gerry McGeer, was brought in to point out the fallacy of Aberhart's theories, but he was howled off the platform; Professor Henry Angus of the University of British Columbia stumped Alberta trying to demonstrate the economic nonsense in Social Credit, but he had no success. Every daily newspaper and most of the weekly press in the province fought Aberhart's crusade, but to no avail. Aberhart became a martyr as well as a saviour.

When the ballots were counted Social Credit had won a resounding victory. The Social Credit party had not only nominated more candidates than the UFA, they had won 54 percent of the vote, 89 percent of the seats in the legislature and had wiped out the UFA for good. The United Farmers had failed to win a single seat. The opposition consisted of two Conservatives and five Liberals.

The victory of Social Credit was also a victory for one-party politics. The opposition in Alberta never again had more than a handful of seats in the legislature. By 1935 Alberta had known one-party rule almost since the inception of the province in 1905.

Social Credit, as a movement, put a further nail in the coffin of normal party politics. As led by Aberhart and described by his followers, it was a religious crusade on behalf of the little people against the financial giants. Those who opposed it had neither compassion nor faith and were among the wicked of the world.

The United Farmers had conditioned the people of Alberta to a political system that was subject to direct influence from the people more than other governments in Canada. This influence was brought to bear through the UFA annual conventions. As a result, Albertans had come to consider that the government was their government—that it should work for them. Direct involvement in politics as a matter-of-fact, day-to-day affair was accepted. When times were bad the people were at once more demanding and more critical of their government. Albertans found much in social credit policy that struck a sympathetic chord in the light of their UFA experience.

Against this background, and with the important ingredients of Aberhart's charismatic personality and his skilful use of radio

William Aberhart addressing an election rally. E. C. Manning is on the right.

and oratory, the Social Credit party filled a need felt by many Albertans. Professor John Irving summed the process up in this manner:

> The social context, the desire for meaning, and the prospect of satisfying their needs combined to produce in Albertans a psychological condition in which they were extremely open to the appeal of Social Credit. At the same time most of them lacked sufficient knowledge of philosophy and the social sciences to enable them to assess its claim to be *the* authentic interpretation of their world. Unable to deal with Social Credit in any critical way, thousands of people accepted it because it brought order into their confused world. They were at once bewildered and had the will to believe. They were in a condition of readiness to respond, and the philosophy of Social Credit lent itself admirably to short-cut rationalizations in the form of slogans and symbols.[11]

*　　*　　*

From 1935 until the time of this writing, Social Credit in Alberta was never in difficulty; indeed, it went from strength to strength, particularly under the leadership of E. C. Manning, Aberhart's successor. Manning also continued the operation of the Bible Institute or, as it became, the Calgary Gospel Tabernacle. The Sunday afternoon sermons of the Alberta Premier remain to this day an institution in many prairie homes.

Chapter VIII

Practice and the Preacher

When it came to power in Alberta, Social Credit was purely provincial in scope. The ideas of Major Douglas had been presented to the federal House of Commons Committee on Banking and Commerce in 1923 by Douglas himself, but they had had little impact. When Aberhart established his party he had no plans for a national version. Unlike the CCF, in which some of the founding impetus came from federal Members of Parliament, and in which the purpose was to establish a *national* movement of provincially based parties, Social Credit started out as a provincial party. It now appears, to a great extent, to have remained so. It spread to other provinces, notably to British Columbia, but not as branches of a single entity. In each case it was an independent provincial party. The same was true with the unsuccessful national Social Credit party. It drew its strength from those provinces in which the provincial movement was strong, but it had no formal ties with the provincial parties. Frequently, as a matter of fact, these various groups were at odds with each other.

THE PHENOMENON IN ALBERTA

The Alberta party of William Aberhart was the first flowering of social credit in Canada. The parties that followed were undoubtedly seeded from this plant, but they grew or died separately, connnected in no formal way with the parent.

With the possible exception of the Quebec Social Credit party of Réal Caouette, in no other province was the response to social credit so overwhelming or so personal as in Alberta. In Alberta it came not as a political doctrine that people found attractive or interesting, but rather as a revelation that changed people's attitudes and, in some cases, their whole outlook on life. The response had all the characteristics of mass hysteria; countless people found that social credit came into their lives with the force of religious conversion. For some it was like the miraculous cure of a long, debilitating illness. An impression of this response can be gained from the interviews with dedicated followers that were reported by Professor Irving in his study of the Social Credit movement in Alberta. A clerk in a department store said:

> I had lost my job as the result of the depression and was down and out, feeling pretty sorry for myself. I used to feel so tired out that I would fall asleep over the newspaper after supper. Then I heard Mr. Aberhart expound Social Credit at the Bible Institute. He made me see why we had a depression. He told us we could end it if we all pulled together. So I decided to take up Social Credit and work for Mr. Aberhart. An amazing change took place. After Social Credit came into my life, I had plenty of pep and energy. It was amazing.[1]

A farmer described how he jumped up at a political meeting and cried out, "Let us pray for Mr. Aberhart!"[2] and how, as everyone prayed, their eyes filled with tears. A school teacher believed that "if we are to fulfil God's purpose for man, we must all take up Social Credit."[3] A small-town businessman was convinced that Aberhart was a "God-inspired man" who would, "solve the problems of the common man forever."[4]

The fantastic, if not fanatical, devotion which the man and the movement inspired had the same effect, only greater in magnitude, as that which has already been described in relation to Woodsworth and the CCF. Aberhart could rely upon hundreds of dedicated and willing workers to carry the message of his movement throughout the province. He could also count on their financial support. Even though the newspapers in the province were against him and all orthodox economists, bankers and businessmen proclaimed the impossibility and irrelevance of his schemes, the people of Alberta were behind him, convinced he had all the answers. The day after the election a number of people lined up outside Social Credit headquarters in Calgary to collect their twenty-five dollar dividends.

Cartoonist Arch Dale's view of Aberhart's "Funny Money" scheme.

Unlike those who stormed the walls of privilege for the CCF in Saskatchewan, the Social Credit regiment was composed not of community leaders—for the most part they remained loyal to the UFA. It was instead an army of the little men, the ordinary people. Many had never been involved in political organization before, but they flocked to Aberhart's banner. There was no intellectual wing of the Social Credit party similar to the League for Social Reconstruction in the CCF, nor was there any support from the leaders of organized labour. It was a movement of the lower middle class, the *petit bourgeoisie*, of people not normally active in any sort of public body but driven by despair and drawn by Aberhart's conviction to the ranks of Social Credit.

The depression had created chaos and bewilderment in Alberta. Hard working farmers could not understand why they got nothing for their crops, or why the shops in the towns and cities were crammed with goods that no one could buy. Aberhart's brand of social credit explained the deficiencies of the system in terms they understood, in terms that exonerated them of any responsibility, laying all the blame at the feet of the financiers. He proposed a solution that was thoroughly consistent with the attitudes of the farmers as small businessmen. The entire package was wrapped in his unimpeachable credentials as a preacher of the gospel. Few of his followers knew much about social credit theory beyond the platitudes of the "A plus B theorem" and the "monetization of the province's resources"—but then Aberhart was not very knowledgeable either. But the details did not matter, as long as the light came on when you pushed the switch. The "experts" would take care of the complicated details.

SOCIAL CREDIT IN POWER

Although the Social Credit party was in power, it was some time before social credit practice came to Alberta, and then it only stayed a short time. Shortly after the election Aberhart sent a telegram to Major Douglas saying, "Victorious when can you come?"[5] Douglas gave Aberhart a date but he was never sent a specific invitation. Next the Alberta Premier asked him for "directions." These Douglas sent. But Aberhart ignored the proposals for "immediate action" which the originator of social credit sent him. Instead, he embarked upon a course that was nothing if not orthodox. The reason Aberhart was unwilling to introduce social credit measures was simple: as Premier of the province he had to govern and to do so he needed money. To get money he had to rely on outside finance. Therefore, he had to ignore the advice of the "founder."

Eighteen months after the Social Credit landslide no social credit measures had been introduced in Alberta. There were no dividends of twenty-five dollars and there was still a good deal of poverty in the midst of plenty. When the 1937 budget was introduced it was a model of financial orthodoxy. To a number of the Social Credit members of the legislature this was tantamount to betrayal. In March an MLA denounced Aberhart and his legislation as the very opposite of social credit. Aberhart, as was his custom, tried to ignore the unrest in the legislature, and appealed to the people of the province over the radio. But the elected members were not to be overcome. As a result of their pressure, the government finally introduced the Alberta Social Credit Act, which included the establishment of a commission to operate a social credit system and the setting up of credit houses to distribute the credit that was to be created under the act. It was not quite what Douglas would have done, but it was near enough to satisfy the rebels.

This adventure into the practice of social credit was short-lived. All the major legislation enacted under the direction of the Social Credit Commission ran afoul of the Canadian constitution and was either reserved by the Lieutenant-Governor and disallowed by the federal government, or declared *ultra vires* by the courts. The Alberta government attempted to distribute its own money ("prosperity certificates" based on the "unused capacity" of the province); it attempted to regulate banks, and control the press; but in each case there was conflict with the Canadian constitution. No fewer than eight Social Credit bills were disallowed by the federal cabinet. By 1939 it was clear to most observers that there would be no social credit in Alberta—nor in any other province for that matter.

Ironically, social credit theory helped preserve the dominance of the men who failed to implement it. From the beginning Aberhart had had little use for the legislature; he much preferred to have matters thrashed out in the secrecy of the party caucus. From 1935 until 1939 he made but one speech in the Alberta house. He pointed out that while the rooster makes all the noise, it is the hen who quietly does the job. The legislature was made subordinate to the cabinet, in a fashion demonstrated earlier by the UFA; in social credit theory this was justified on the ground that the cabinet members were the "experts." The same was also true for the party rank and file. They were told at their convention by Aberhart and Manning that they should only concern themselves with general aims; discussion of detailed matters was outside their competence. Thus, the cabinet emerged as supreme. With the failure of social credit practice there were no experts outside the cabinet, and the cabinet had clearly established its sup·riority over the legislature and the party convention.

Social Credit had come into prominence in Alberta as a champion of the people against the "vested interests". But by 1939 the people were less influential than they had been in 1935 and the government was no less orthodox and a good deal more dictatorial. There was, however, never any open disavowal by the party of social credit theory. Although nothing further was done to introduce social credit measures after 1939, Manning, Aberhart and their followers were still ardent advocates of social credit philosophy. They had, they insisted, been frustrated by the "small group of international money monopolists" who controlled the Ottawa government. [6] For the more rabid social crediters, those who had followed the evolution of Douglas' thought, these monopolists represented an international conspiracy of Jews to control the world economy. Until the Alberta party split in 1949, these people, who kept their belief in social credit alight with the fuel of anti-semitism, remained in the Social Credit party.

The war and the prosperity that came with the resurgence of successful oil exploration served to remove the problems that had made social credit theories attractive. But the governing Social Credit party still professed its belief in the theory, if not the practice. The administration of Alberta's affairs was orthodox,

Premier Ernest Manning of Alberta contemplates the future of Canada at the Confederation of Tomorrow conference, 1968. He announced his retirement from office late the same year.

sympathetic to free enterprise and conservative, with occasional overtones of small-mindedness, insularity and anti-intellectualism. Nevertheless, it suited the people and the entrepreneurs well enough.

Aberhart died in 1943, and Ernest C. Manning succeeded him as premier. Under Manning the government of Alberta was a businessman's government. Decisions were made by the cabinet, there was no nonsense, and no time was wasted on unnecessary debate. The people of the province clearly appreciated this kind of administration. Apart from a slight slump in 1940—due to some disillusionment over the failure to bring in social credit— the government enjoyed lavish majorities in the provincial house. The quest for Douglasite prosperity was shelved; oil and free enterprise succeeded where the "monetization of unused capacity" and the "A plus B theorem" had not. Beneath the umbrella of oil royalties and American capital investment all things seemed possible. The enemy-in-chief became socialism. As Professor Macpherson points out:

> The menace of socialism became and remained the staple of the official Alberta social credit propaganda.[7]

In fact, the official Social Credit magazine suggested that the old enemy—"banking monopoly"—had been in league with the socialists all along.

OUTSIDE ALBERTA

Unlike socialism, social credit did not become a viable national force. The national Social Credit party, led between 1944 and 1958 by Solon Low, a former Alberta cabinet minister, failed to establish itself in any province outside of Alberta to the extent that the CCF did. In 1935 seventeen Social Credit MP's were elected to the federal House, fifteen from Alberta and two from Saskatchewan. In 1940 only ten Social Crediters were returned, all from Alberta, and in 1945 thirteen, again all from Alberta. The party managed to win four seats in British Columbia in the 1953 election, but it still failed to achieve the status of a national party. Outside Alberta, British Columbia and possibly Saskatchewan, it had no real organization and performed dismally at the polls. In 1962, however, under the fiery leadership of Réal Caouette, the Quebec Social Credit party sprang into prominence, sending twenty-six MP's to Ottawa. But this success was short-lived. With no real possibility of forming a government, and feeding only on the rancour and bitterness of the *petit bourgeois Quebecois*, Caouette's movement appeared to decline, although it continued to attract interest in some parts of the province and to elect supporters to the federal House of Commons.

By 1968 the national Social Credit party was in disarray and total decline. In 1967 E. C. Manning had published a book in which he urged a regrouping of the right wing political forces in Canada to stave off the growing trend, as he saw it, toward socialism. Although he refused to involve himself personally in federal politics, Manning was anxious to redress the balance between left and right in Canada. The same year saw Robert Thompson resign as national leader of the party. In 1968 Thompson, with Manning's endorsement, ran in the federal general election as a Progressive Conservative. Thompson's defection appeared to mark the formal demise of the national Social Credit party. A few candidates ran under the national party label in 1968 but none were elected.

If success was denied Social Credit on the national level, it was attained in one province other than Alberta. In 1952 the newly formed British Columbia Social Credit League became the government of British Columbia under the leadership of William Andrew Cecil Bennett, an ex-Conservative MLA.

In 1941 the CCF in British Columbia had won more votes than either the Conservatives or Liberals, although not enough to form a government. The two old parties had, therefore, decided to combine their forces in a coalition to resist the CCF advance. By 1952 the coalition government had lost favour. If not corrupt, it was inefficient and inept. In particular, the voters in the interior of the province considered themselves ill-treated by the government, and with some justification.

The Social Credit party had contested one or two seats in earlier provincial elections, but with noticeable lack of success. In the 1952 campaign, with some assistance from Alberta and some amateur help, the party surprised everyone, including its members, by winning nineteen seats. This was one more than the CCF and a lot more than the four seats won by the Conservatives or the six won by the Liberals. The platform was not Douglas social credit; it was not even Alberta social credit. It was nothing more than the promise of good, honest, middle-of-the-road government, with special attention to the needs of the masses in the interior. For the position of premier, the most obvious choice was the renegade Tory, W. A. C. Bennett.

Equipped with boundless self-confidence and all the energy and daring of the pure amateur, Bennett's Social Credit government proceeded to "get things done." A massive highway building program was launched, existing programs were streamlined, and the government moved from success to success. Freely admitting that he knew nothing about social credit theory and could not care less, the Premier pursued a vigorous free enterprise policy, with the government playing the part of a major entrepreneur. If Bennett had one guideline it was that of expediency.

This enabled him to take over private ferry operations in the province and establish one of the world's largest publicly-owned ferry fleets. Later, when it suited his purposes, the government took over the private power company, the B.C. Electric, all the while vigorously denouncing the socialist policies of the CCF opposition. The appeal of Bennett's government was its productivity, profitability and plausibility. All around them the people of the province were able to see—and feel if they chose—the works of the government, from paved roads to huge dams.

Bennett paid even less attention to the British Columbia Social Credit League than E. C. Manning accorded his party in Alberta. The annual conventions of the League were treated by the party leaders as irrelevant. The resolutions passed were ignored. Cabinet ministers seldom attended and the Premier himself only appeared to make the major address. The League was ornamental and, like most ornaments, of little use. The Legislature was also considered grossly inefficient. Too much talk and too little action was the Premier's description. To the members of the opposition parties, the annual sessions became exercises in frustration. The government ignored the usual customs of parliamentary practice and reduced the Legislature to impotence by consistently refusing to provide answers to questions or the kind of information needed by opposition parties if they are to perform their proper function.

Unlike the Alberta government, however, British Columbia Social Credit was not assured a minuscule opposition. The Conservative party disappeared from the provincial house after 1953 and the Liberals were reduced to a corporal's guard of four, but the CCF managed to retain roughly 25 percent of the seats. In fact, the combined opposition parties always won more than 50 percent of the popular vote in provincial elections. In Alberta the Social Credit party seldom won less than 50 percent.

The difference between Alberta and British Columbia can best be accounted for by the different natures of the two provinces. British Columbia was not a rural province; its population was concentrated in the lower corner of the province, in Vancouver and Victoria. The provincial economies also differed; while based on primary production like Alberta's, British Columbia's economy was concerned with the production of raw materials by employees, not farm produce by producer-owners. There was a large labouring population in British Columbia, highly unionized and generally radical in political outlook. From the time it was formed in 1933 the CCF in British Columbia seldom got less than 30 percent of the popular vote. British Columbia was, in fact, one of the strongholds of the CCF in national terms.

Social Credit's success in British Columbia can be accounted for by its skill in running the province as a successful business would be run—at a profit and with good service to the customer. Faced with a choice between Social Credit or socialism, enough of the voters chose Social Credit in each election to ensure Premier Bennett a long career as managing director of the province.

A CONTINUING EXPRESSION OF WESTERN OPINION

By 1952 Social Credit in the west was no longer a vehicle of protest—it was an engine for protection of the *status quo*. It offered results, not theories; sound business practice, not schemes of socialist planners. Conditions were such that people wanted to hold on to—and if possible add to—the benefits prosperity had brought them. Social Credit seemed to provide the conditions that would permit them to do so.

There was no longer any widespread unrest in the west. The depression was only a bitter memory, and at that only for older people. By 1960 the discontent that had brought forth protest had been transformed into prosperity. There was no need to oppose the *status quo*, to vilify the money barons or to damn the party system. In Alberta there was no party system anyway, and in British Columbia party politics did not matter very much. There were some who still believed fervently in Douglasite social credit doctrine—and some of these were even in government. But few people took such ideas seriously. Like antique furniture, they were retained as curious reminders of the past but never used, partly out of respect and partly through fear that they might collapse under the weight of reality.

The legacy of William Aberhart's movement, if any legacy there is, can be found in these two governments and in a tradition of isolation and disdain for the party system and acceptable parliamentary practice. For example, at a time when the Quebec separatist movement was strong, Premier Bennett displayed less interest in Canada than many a French-Canadian separatist. His frequent vocal assaults on Ottawa were matched by the vigour with which his government pursued provincial rights and autonomy in such diverse areas as the Columbia River treaty with the United States, the question of off-shore mineral rights, and the construction and administration of a "super-port" south of Vancouver. Characteristically, the Social Credit government of British Columbia planned to spend more than four times as much on its pavilion at the Japanese fair at Osaka as it had spent on the province's participation in Expo 67 celebrating the Centennial of Canada.

To some extent Premier Bennett's use of the federal authority as a straw man was the product of political ingenuity, for it enabled the Premier to portray himself as the champion of his people. But it was equally true that behind the persistent criticism lay the westerner's distrust of the east, of a government which, Mr. Bennett claimed, took more in taxes from British Columbia than it gave back in services and grants. In fact, of course, this characterization of the federal government was not true. Moreover, as British Columbia was the second wealthiest province, her wealth was needed to help in the maintenance of less well endowed provinces. Nevertheless, Bennett's argument was simple and unsophisticated and, accordingly, of political utility. It was also an argument consistent with the old threads of Social Credit, Aberhart style.

Premier Manning was less abrupt in his manner than Bennett and was felt by many to have demonstrated a greater awareness of the Canadian identity. The contrast was clearly evident during the Federal-Provincial Conference of 1967. It opened to a chorus from the press that implied the toughest premiers would be those from Quebec and the three western provinces. Manning was a reluctant participant in discussions concerning French language and other rights, but by the time the conference concluded he had demonstrated a willingness to compromise that had not been expected. Bennett, for his part, saw the conference merely as a platform from which to state British Columbia's grievances, and he departed before it was over. Ross Thatcher, Liberal Premier of Saskatchewan, was only slightly more co-operative than his neighbours. He too demonstrated the western apprehension of eastern designs.

It would have been surprising if, after decades of opposition to, and little succour from, the east, the western provinces had demonstrated any great depth of feeling toward the east and those politicians who had traditionally been accused of little concern for the agony and hardship of the western frontier. The mistrust—if not hostility—grows and deepens as the distance from Ottawa increases in a westerly direction. Distance is not the sole cause, but the record of the past and the diminution of full communication that distance produces have both served to support the claims of those politicians who wish to perpetuate the bogey of eastern insensitivity and desire to dominate. What was in origin a real problem of vast proportions, one very largely related to agriculture, is now more and more a myth perpetuated largely for partisan reasons. Although the west did, to a great extent, win the battle, a residue of hostility and suspicion remains.

*   *   *

Social Credit, emerging as little more than a label for what were essentially conservative governments, seemed to typify a situation some writers have described as "the end of ideology." According to many Social Crediters, the old debates between left and right were no longer relevant. The acceptance of

Keynesian economics, the growth of the welfare state, the continuation of prosperity, all seemed to indicate that government was less a matter of ideas in conflict and more a matter of successful administration. For Premier Bennett in British Columbia, a man's political label mattered little; the question was, could he do the job? If he could, there was a place for him in the government. The traditional debate between socialism and free enterprise became something of an election gimmick, and the government clearly refused to accept the distinction in its own activities. In British Columbia and Alberta social credit became a synonym for right-of-centre pragmatism. Success and prosperity diminish the validity of ideology. Premiers Manning and Bennett did not ask their electorates to judge their philosophies; they asked only if the people thought they were doing a good job. It is clear that a good many people thought so.

While the Liberal and Conservative parties in the two westernmost provinces suffered grievously from electoral malnutrition, when they spoke to the public they could do little more than insist that they could do a better job. On the other hand, the CCF and later the NDP tried to argue that it could do a different job, and that ideological differences were still important. For the socialist party such a distinction is a matter of life and death for, if the only real distinction is proficiency in administration, the socialist has to use the same arguments as his Liberal or Conservative counterparts. For the socialist party the ultimate goals, which are based on an ideological point of view, remain unaltered, although the means of achieving them have changed and much of the early zeal of the movement has disappeared.

Chapter IX

Parliament and Protest

The institutions of parliamentary government presume fairly settled attitudes and habits of political behaviour. Almost all commentators have pointed out that parliament works best with two parties—one as government and the other as opposition. In Canada the two major parties have always subscribed to this view, for obvious reasons. The idea that government is most effectively carried on when the people are represented by two parties assumes that there are really only two points of view; for example, people are either liberal or conservative, or conservative or labour. The old parties insist that the existence of three or more parties is only confusing and leads to inefficiency. Proposals for electoral reform in Canada are always attacked if it seems that they would lead to a more permanent multi-party system.

PROTEST AS AN EFFECTIVE POLITICAL WEAPON

In fact, Canada has had a multi-party system since 1921, when the Progressives first appeared in the west. Admittedly, none of the "other" parties has managed to form the government, but they have on occasion attracted significant support. What is more important, they have exerted considerable influence by the mere fact of their presence. A politician is concerned with nothing so much as he is with staying in office. Threats to his political power or that of his party as the government elicit his rapt attention and usually produce great activity to meet the challenge.

The implication of such a response appears to be lust for power and jealousy of rivals—the standard sins attributed to politicians. No politician is free from ambition; why would anyone undertake such an arduous career if he were not ambitious? But it is foolish to argue, as some have, that a politician is only interested in power. They have goals like most people; they have ideas they wish to implement and power is the means of implementing them. Most politicians have a strong sense of duty, of public service. It is difficult to separate the various strands in anyone's character, and folly to try; it is equally foolish to look for a single dominant trait that will explain everything.

A politician will respond to threats to his position for a variety of reasons, the chief of which is his determination to stay in power or to maintain the position from which he hopes to achieve power. Because of this, the protest movements were able to achieve results that could not have been achieved unless they had had power themselves. Mackenzie King moved his party to the left, much to the chagrin of a number of his party's financial backers, in order to counter the threat posed by the CCF. Earlier he had introduced reform measures to undermine the support of the Progressives, and to make the Liberal party more attractive to Progressive MP's. King's successor Louis St. Laurent, said of the CCF that they were simply "Liberals in a hurry," implying that what they proposed was not bad, only premature.

MULTI-PARTY POLITICS IN CANADA

For simplicity, the idea of a two-party system takes the prize. But it is too simple. In a country as small as Britain, with the homogeneity of outlook and ease of communication she enjoys, it is perhaps more workable. But in Canada, with our vast spaces, scattered population, variety of population centres and, most important of all, federal constitution, it is clearly unworkable. The disappearance of a "pure" two-party system began with the expansion of Canada's population and the development of the western provinces. The people living at extreme distances from Ottawa, Montreal and Toronto—the real centres of power and influence—soon came to appreciate the disadvantages of isolation and political insignificance.

The two old parties were based in the east, financed by the east and controlled by the east. For the people in the west this meant frustration and unrest: they had neither the arm nor the ear of the ruling parties. It was thoroughly consistent with the frontier tradition of self-sufficiency and independence that they should form their own political machines to influence or wrest power from the old and insensitive engines of government in the east. Their economic situation also placed them in the position of vassals to the eastern potentates of the CPR, Massey-Harris, and other large firms that set prices, held mortgages and, to a large extent, influenced governments. This factor gave further impetus to the development of indigenous parties and movements in the west.

Out of the tensions created by the combination of a federal constitution with a parliamentary system of government, there arose the kind of multi-party system Canada now has. It is actually one in which two multi-party systems coexist and intermingle, while remaining distinct. At the federal level one can find three parties, five if one includes the varieties of Social Credit. At the provincial level each province has its own peculiarities. In Ontario there are three parties. Quebec has four but, unlike any of the other provinces, no Conservative party; instead there is the *Union Nationale*, a purely provincial party. In British Columbia the Conservative party is moribund and Social Credit is in power, with the NDP and Liberals in opposition. During federal elections the provincial parties usually help their national confreres—indeed, the personnel are frequently the same. In some provinces, however, such co-operation is restrained or non-existent. In short, we have a complex multi-party system at two levels.

Within a parliamentary system, no single party can represent the diverse interests of a federal state. In Canada successive prime ministers have attempted to provide regional representation within the cabinet, a minimum of one minister being taken from each province when possible, with Quebec and Ontario having the same number—usually four or five. It has also been customary to give the Agriculture portfolio to a prairie MP, the Fisheries to a member from one of the coastal provinces, Finance to Ontario, and so on. But this system really does not work. Within the context of such traditional practices of parliamentary government as cabinet solidarity, the predominance of the prime minister and strict party unity, it has been difficult to give adequate representation to all regions, particularly when the party in power has been dominated by interests based in Ontario and Quebec. The system has alleviated some tensions but it has not removed them. A man is no less subject to the pressures of the party bosses simply because he is from Saskatchewan.

The radicals knew this, and the Progressive attack on the

party system went to the heart of the matter. Sending a man to Ottawa in the Liberal or Conservative party guaranteed only that he would soon become a member of the rank and file drilled by eastern party officials. The only way they could ensure that their views were fairly represented was to send their own men to Ottawa with their own label. They did not realize that whether they came to power or not, their very presence would cause the old parties to look more closely at the west and to respond with more zeal to the needs of the farmers—not because the old parties suddenly saw the problems, but because they recognized the challenge to their dominance. When that happened the problems assumed an importance they had hitherto lacked.

The Winnipeg general strike awakened a similar realization among many trade unionists. The response of the leading figures in the community and the reaction of the Borden government demonstrated clearly that trade unionism was neither understood nor accepted by the established leaders of Canadian society. The isolation of the trade unionist was as great as, if not greater than, that of the farmer, but it was less easily corrected for not being geographical. The social and political ostracism of the trade union movement was nation-wide and, ultimately, drove the trade union movement to engage in third-party activity in order either to form a government of men sympathetic to their aims, or to influence existing parties so as to exact from them guarantees and protection for union activities. The existing parties, nourished by the "establishment" in eastern Canada, were singularly unresponsive to trade union needs. This was understandable, for some of the major figures in both parties were industrialists whose hatred of unions was exquisite. As the sociologist, John Porter, has shown, unions existed by permission, not by right.

In a system dominated by parties that were themselves dominated by a particular segment or class of Canadian society, it is small wonder that the diversity of the country, which led to the federal system, failed to be adequately represented. To those outside the power structure it made little difference who was in office, Liberals or Conservatives—although it happened to be Liberals most of the time—because both parties were largely representative of, and responsive to, only one segment of society. It was, to be sure, not a small segment, nor was it only a minority;

indeed, the attitudes enshrined in the policies of the two old parties have reflected a fairly dominant point of view right across Canada. But, and this is the nub of the argument, it was a point of view that excluded significant minority economic and social groups. Furthermore, the parliamentary system made adequate representation of these groups impossible within the the framework of a two-party system.

THE WEST—A UNIQUE SITUATION

If the combination of federalism and the parliamentary system was a major factor in the rise of protest movements, why were such movements largely confined to the western plains? Surely one could have expected similar developments in the perennially depressed areas of Canada—the Maritime provinces. The locale of the protest movements is an indication that there were other factors involved. There was the difference of expectation. The settlers of the prairies had gone to the west filled with high hopes of a prosperous, independent, self-sufficient existence. Like many men before and after, they believed implicitly in the agrarian myth of the solid honesty, purity and rewarding nature of the rural life. Life was supposed to be good in the west. To the people of the Maritimes, on the other hand, marginal living was accepted as inevitable. The depression certainly brought additional hardship, but it was relatively less severe than that visited upon the west. The Maritimers' expectations were not those of the new settlers in the west and their political attitudes were based on settled habits and inherited preferences. When one is hip-deep in mud, another inch or so makes little difference; but the man who is dry-shod expresses concern when he steps into a puddle.

Agrarian life on the prairie was not what many settlers had expected. Wheat farming is unlike mixed farming. In Ontario a farmer could sell his produce locally. He could live on it himself to some extent, and he could earn a reasonable income from a relatively small farm. But in Saskatchewan, wheat was king. It required not acres but sections. It could only be marketed through the grain exchange, and mostly on the world market. The wheat farmer could not live off his own produce exclusively. From the beginning he faced higher costs, greater risks and had less control over his income. He had come to depend upon outside help to make his living. He demanded more of the government because there was much he could not do for himself.

In addition, many of the men who homesteaded in the west came from Britain or the United States. Many were familiar with the ideas of the British socialists, or the American agrarian radicals. Many of the ideas of the Progressives came from below the border; Henry Wise Wood, for example, was an American. The CCF reflected the ideas of British socialism. And social credit was, of course, the product of Major C. H. Douglas' fertile imagination, although in this case the British seed was sown in ground already tilled by the ideas of American progressivism and populism.

THE IMPORTANCE OF LEADERSHIP

Because he was an individualist, frustrated in his ambitions, the prairie farmer was prepared to take action. Because he needed positive government assistance he was prepared to engage in political activity. Because he suspected, not without cause, those engaged in business and finance, he was prepared to reform politics to overcome the pernicious influences on politics exercised by such institutions as the large corporations. And because he came to know the value of co-operation amidst the alien vastness of the prairie, he was attracted to those ideas that opposed competition and gave primacy to group activity. The farmer was prepared to follow those whose words and deeds manifested the ideals he believed in. Thus, men like James Shaver Woodsworth, Henry Wise Wood, Robert Gardiner, William Irvine, George Williams, E. A. Partridge and William Aberhart were able to muster a following strong enough to leave a deep imprint on Canadian politics.

The leadership ability of an individual is clearly a significant factor in history. The pervasive influence of the Duke of Wellington, the roles played by men like Napoleon, Churchill, or John Kennedy, are crucial to an understanding of the history of the times. But no man builds a following from thin air. Leadership, a sociologist would say, is largely situational. That is, one cannot lead unless the conditions are such that people are ready to follow that kind of leadership. Churchill was summarily dismissed by the British people immediately the war was over.

John F. Kennedy would almost certainly have been defeated by Dwight Eisenhower had they been running against each other.

In the case of the men and movements discussed in these pages, leadership was a factor, particularly in the case of Woodsworth and Aberhart. Both were associated with religion; both were teachers; both took up the defense of the individual against the big interests. Aberhart inspired his followers by the force of his oratory and the skill of his presentation. By mastering the techniques of radio and using them to full advantage, he reached thousands he would otherwise have been unable to touch. Woodsworth was no orator, nor did he have the public relations or organizational cunning of Aberhart; he won followers by the example he set of consistent adherence to high principle. He was revered by his followers; for them, and for many not in the CCF, he was the embodiment of the party's ideals. It would be fair to say that Woodsworth attracted a following while Aberhart built one. Neither, however, would have succeeded to the extent they did had the condition of the times and the temper of the people been other than what they were.

*   *   *

The growth and development of protest movements and the political parties into which they developed, tested the democratic system in Canada and tried the tolerance of Canadian society. Despite the bitterness of propaganda on both sides, the invasion of individual liberties that occasionally occurred and the irrational suspicion that existed of the radicals, these movements and parties continued to exist, free from overt suppression, and they continued to exert an influence on Canadian politics. Engendered by the rigidity of the system, they remained alive because of its ultimate flexibility. If the nature of parliament made them necessary, it was parliament that made them effective. The insensitivity of the political system brought about the welding together of fragmentary dissent to form a concerted demand for reform that was heard and could not be ignored. Farmers and labourers, both separately and together, grappled with the system, shook it and changed it, but did not destroy it. The result was the creation of new parties, the disappearance of the two-party system, and a reassertion of some forgotten aspects of democracy having to do with the representation of all the people.

TIME CHART

First World War begins	**1914**	
	1916	Farmers' Platform published by Canadian Council of Agriculture
Russian Revolution	**1917**	
First World War ends	**1918**	
	1919	One Big Union convention in Calgary
		United Farmers of Ontario form provincial government
		May-July, Winnipeg general strike
	1920	National Progressive Party formed
	1921	Farmers' Party (later the UFA) wins Alberta election
		Mackenzie King's Liberals win federal election; Progressives second with 65 seats
	1923	J. S. Woodsworth and Wm. Irvine form the Labour group in House of Commons
	1924	'Ginger Group' breaks away from Progressives
	1925	Federal election precipitates constitutional crisis (King-Byng-Meighen)
		William Aberhart begins his religious broadcasts over CFCN in Calgary
	1926	Constitutional crisis: Meighen is Prime Minister briefly until defeated in the general election by King. Marks the end of the Progressives
Collapse of New York stock market signals the start of the great depression	**1929**	First conference of the Western Labour Political Parties in Regina
		Depression hits Canada: price of wheat drops by more than 50% between 1929 and 1933; lumber and newsprint down by almost 40% in the same period
	1930	General election: R. B. Bennett forms Conservative government
	1932	William Aberhart discovers Social Credit
		CCF founded in Calgary, J. S. Woodsworth elected leader
Adolf Hitler becomes Chancellor in Germany	**1933**	Over half a million Canadians out of work
	1934	Prime Minister Bennett announces his "New Deal" to help offset the Depression

	1935	Unemployed men begin the Ottawa "trek" General election, Mackenzie King and the Liberal party back in office William Aberhart leads Social Credit to overwhelming victory in Alberta
Second World War begins	**1939**	
	1940	M. J. Coldwell succeeds J. S. Woodsworth as leader of the CCF General Election: King wins again
	1943	Gallup Poll shows CCF with more support than either Liberals or Conservatives CCF wins 39 seats in Ontario election to become official opposition Canadian Congress of Labour endorses CCF as "political arm of labour" Ernest Manning succeeds Aberhart as Social Credit leader in Alberta
	1944	CCF wins election in Saskatchewan to become first socialist government in North America
Second World War ends	**1945**	CCF loses all but 8 seats in Ontario election King and Liberal party win general election
	1948	Louis St. Laurent succeeds Mackenzie King
NATO formed	**1949**	St. Laurent leads Liberals to victory in general election
Korean War	**1950-51**	
	1952	W. A. C. Bennett becomes Social Credit Premier of British Columbia
	1955	Canadian Congress of Labour, and Trades and Labour Congress merge to become Canadian Labour Congress (CLC)
	1957	John Diefenbaker becomes Prime Minister ending 22 years of Liberal domination
Election of J. F. Kennedy as U.S. President	**1960**	
	1961	New Democratic Party formed
	1962	General election: Diefenbaker heads a minority government; Social Credit upsurge in Quebec
President Kennedy assassinated	**1963**	Liberals under Lester Pearson form minority government
	1964	Liberals defeat CCF in Saskatchewan
	1968	Ernest Manning retires as premier of Alberta Pierre Trudeau becomes Prime Minister of Canada

Notes

Chapter I

1. Bruce Hutchison, *The Unknown Country* (Toronto: Longmans, Green, 1942), p. 296.
2. Grant MacEwan, *Between the Red and the Rockies* (Toronto: University of Toronto Press, 1952), p. 235.
3. Vancouver *News Advertiser*, October 14, 1901.
4. K. W. McNaught, *A Prophet in Politics: A Biography of J. S. Woodsworth* (Toronto: University of Toronto Press, 1959), p. 26.
5. Cited in W. L. Morton, *The Progressive Party in Canada* (Toronto: University of Toronto Press, 1950), p. 17, from *The Grain Growers' Guide*, Winnipeg, November 2, 1910, p. 11.
6. *Western Clarion*, May 7, 1903.

Chapter II

1. D. C. Masters, *The Winnipeg General Strike* (Toronto: University of Toronto Press, 1950), p. 4.
2. *Ibid.*, p. 39.
3. *Winnipeg Citizen*, May 21, 1919.
4. Victoria *Daily Colonist*, June 17, 1919.
5. Cited in K. W. McNaught, *A Prophet in Politics: A Biography of J. S. Woodsworth* (Toronto: University of Toronto Press, 1959), p. 124, from House of Commons *Debates*, 1919, pp. 3843 *et seq.*
6. Cited in McNaught, *op. cit.* pp. 125/26.

7. Masters, *op. cit.* pp. 131/32.
8. McNaught, *op. cit.* p. 101.
9. Cited in W. L. Morton, *The Progressive Party in Canada* (Toronto: University of Toronto Press, 1950), pp. 117/18, from *The Grain Growers' Guide*, Winnipeg, May 21, 1919, p. 5.
10. Morton, *op. cit.* pp. 45/6.
11. W. Irvine, *The Farmers in Politics* (Toronto: McClelland and Stewart, 1920), pp. 56/7.
12. Morton, *op. cit.* p. 39.
13. W. K. Rolph, *Henry Wise Wood of Alberta* (Toronto: University of Toronto Press, 1950), pp. 217/18.

Chapter III

1. Cited in W. L. Morton, *The Progressive Party in Canada* (Toronto: University of Toronto Press, 1950), pp. 116/17, from *The Grain Growers' Guide*, Winnipeg, October 5, 1921, p. 27.
2. Morton, *op. cit.* pp. 152/53.
3. Morton, *op. cit.* p. 153.
4. Cited in Morton, *op. cit.* p. 193, from House of Commons *Debates*, 1924, p. 2214.
5. Cited in Morton, *op. cit.* p. 195.
6. Cited in K. W. McNaught, *A Prophet in Politics: A Biography of J. S. Woodsworth* (Toronto: University of Toronto Press, 1959), p. 167.
7. P.A.C., Manuscript in Henry Spencer Papers (n.d.).

Chapter IV

1. Cited in R. C. Brown and M. Prang, *Confederation to 1949* ("Canadian Historical Documents Series", vol. III) (Toronto: Prentice-Hall, 1966), p. 217, from House of Commons *Debates*, March 17, 1921, p. 72.

2. Cited in Brown and Prang, *op. cit.* pp. 230/31, from *Report, The Royal Commission on Price Spreads* (Ottawa: King's Printer, 1937).

3. *Report of the Royal Commission on Dominion-Provincial Relations* ("Rowell-Sirois Report") (Ottawa: King's Printer, 1940), p. 144.

4. G. E. Britnell, *The Wheat Economy* (Toronto: University of Toronto Press, 1939), p. 210.

5. Cited in Brown and Prang, *op. cit.* p. 220.

6. Cited in Brown and Prang, *op. cit.* pp. 222-224, from Ronald Liversedge, *Recollections of the On-to-Ottawa Trek, 1935* (Vancouver: privately printed, n.d.).

7. Cited in Brown and Prang, *op. cit.* p. 225, from Vancouver *Province*, June 22, 1935.

8. P.A.C., CCF Papers, Minutes, 1929 Conference, Western Labour Political Parties.

9. *Ibid.*, 1931 Conference.

10. P.A.C., CCF Papers, *Declaration of Ultimate Objectives*, passed by UFA Convention, 1932.

11. W. L. Morton, *The Progressive Party in Canada* (Toronto: University of Toronto Press, 1950), p. 280.

12. Cited in K. W. McNaught, *A Prophet in Politics: A Biography of J. S. Woodsworth* (Toronto: University of Toronto Press, 1959), p. 249, from House of Commons *Debates*, 1932, pp. 226 *et seq.*

13. The Liberal journalist was Bruce Hutchison, cited in McInnis, *J. S. Woodsworth: A Man to Remember* (Toronto: Macmillan, 1953), p. 320.

Chapter V

1. W. L. Morton, *The Progressive Party in Canada* (Toronto: University of Toronto Press, 1950), p. 282.

2. *The Co-operative Commonwealth Federation, An Outline of Its Origins, Organization and Objectives* (Calgary, 1932).

3. Cited in B. Borsook, "The Workers Hold a Conference", from *Canadian Forum*, XXV, September, 1932.

4. The Regina Manifesto is appended to K. W. McNaught, *A Prophet in Politics: A Biography of J. S. Woodsworth* (Toronto: University of Toronto Press, 1959).

5. P.A.C., CCF Papers, CCF Pamphlet, 1940.

6. *Ibid.*

7. McNaught, *op. cit.* p. 311.

8. *Ibid.*, p. 309.

Chapter VI

1. S. M. Lipset, *Agrarian Socialism* (Berkeley: University of California Press, 1959), pp. 176/77.

2. J. W. Pickersgill, *The Mackenzie King Record*, Vol. I: *1939-44* (Toronto: University of Toronto Press, 1960), p. 601.

3. *Ibid.*, p. 649.

4. R. Graham, *Arthur Meighen*, Vol. III: *No Surrender* (Toronto: Clarke, Irwin, 1965). p. 153.

5. S. Jamieson, *Industrial Relations in Canada* (Toronto: Macmillan 1957), p. 95.

6. P.A.C., CCF Papers, Winnipeg Declaration, reprinted in Leo Zakuta, *A Protest Movement Becalmed* (Toronto: University of Toronto Press, 1964).

Chapter VII

1. C. B. Macpherson, *Democracy in Alberta* (Toronto: University of Toronto Press, 2nd ed., 1962), p. 106.

2. *Ibid.*, p. 119.
3. *Ibid.*, p. 144.
4. J. A. Irving, *The Social Credit Movement in Alberta:* (Toronto: University of Toronto Press, 1959), p. 29.
5. *Ibid.*, p. 57.
6. *Ibid.*, p. 90.
7. Macpherson, *op. cit.*, p. 146.
8. *Ibid.*, p. 152.
9. Irving, *op. cit.*, p. 316.
10. *Ibid.*, p. 317.
11. *Ibid.*, p. 337.

Chapter VIII

1. J. A. Irving, *The Social Credit Movement in Alberta* (Toronto: University of Toronto Press, 1959), p. 267.
2. *Ibid.*, p. 262.
3. *Ibid.*, p. 261.
4. *Ibid.*, p. 201.
5. *Ibid.*, p. 333.
6. C. B. Macpherson, *Democracy in Alberta* (Toronto: University of Toronto Press, 2nd ed., 1962), p. 201.
7. *Ibid.*, p. 206.

Bibliographical Note

Useful for the whole period under discussion in this volume are two collections of historical documents: R. Craig Brown and Margaret Prang (eds.), *Canadian Historical Documents Series*, vol. III (Toronto: Prentice-Hall, 1966); and Stewart Reid, Kenneth McNaught and Harry Crowe (eds.), *A Source-Book of Canadian History* (Toronto, Longmans, 1959).

For the development of the social gospel and western radicalism: Kenneth McNaught's biography of J. S. Woodsworth, *A Prophet in Politics* (Toronto: University of Toronto Press, 1959), is particularly good as are the early chapters of W. L. Morton, *The Progressive Party in Canada* (Toronto: University of Toronto Press, 1950). The standard work on British Columbia is Margaret Ormsby, *British Columbia: A History* (Toronto: Macmillan, 1958). The most succinct economic summary of the nation's development during this period is in volume I of the Rowell-Sirois Report, *The Report of the Royal Commission on Dominion-Provincial Relations* (Ottawa: King's Printer, 1940). On the economy of the prairies, the two standard works are G. Britnell, *The Wheat Economy* (Toronto: University of Toronto Press, 1939) and Vernon Fowke, *The National Policy and the Wheat Economy* (Toronto: University of Toronto Press, 1957). John Porter discusses at some length social attitudes toward trade unionism and radical politics in *The Vertical Mosaic* (Toronto: University of Toronto Press, 1965). The novels and short stories of Sinclair Ross and Frederick Philip Grove provide a good picture of life on the plains during this period; this is particularly so of Ross' *As for Me and My House* (Toronto: McClelland and Stewart, 1958) and his short story "Cornet at Night" in *Lamp at Noon and Other Stories* (Toronto: McClelland and Stewart, 1968); G. MacEwan's *Between the Red and the Rockies* (Toronto: University of Toronto Press, 1952) is another useful study.

The Winnipeg general strike is discussed at some length in McNaught's biography of Woodsworth, and in detail in D. C. Masters, *The Winnipeg General Strike* (Toronto: University of Toronto Press, 1950). W. L. Morton's study of the Progressive party is a standard source while W. K. Rolph's *Henry Wise Wood of Alberta* (Toronto: University of Toronto Press, 1950) is particularly useful for the development of the UFA and the philosophy of group government. Paul Sharp, *The Agrarian Revolt in Western Canada* (Minneapolis: University of Minnesota Press, 1945) provides a good indication of the American sources of influence, particularly the Non-Partisan League. The *Canadian Annual Review* is invaluable for selections of contemporary opinion of the major events.

For Chapter III the major source is, obviously, Morton's *The Progressive Party in Canada* (Toronto: University of Toronto Press, 1950). In addition volume two of the Mackenzie King biography by Blair Neatby is valuable, as is McNaught's *A Prophet in Politics*. The best treatment of the constitutional crisis is Eugene Forsey, *The Royal Power of Dissolution of Parliament in the British Commonwealth* (Toronto: Oxford University Press, 1943). Another side of the crisis is in volume two of Roger Graham's biography of Arthur Meighen, *Fortune Fled* (Toronto: Clarke, Irwin, 1963). A most useful handbook on the working of the parliamentary system of government in Canada is J. Saywell and J. Ricker, *How Are We Governed?* (Toronto: Clarke, Irwin, 1961); a more detailed treatment, particularly of parties and parliament, is the Norman Ward edition of R. M. Dawson, *The Government of Canada* (Toronto: University of Toronto Press, 1963).

The history of the depression is outlined in volume I of the Rowell-Sirois *Report*. A lucid analysis of the same event in the United States is J. K. Galbraith's *The Great Crash* (Boston: Houghton, Mifflin, 1929). A useful guide to attitudes in Canada at the time are the back issues of *Canadian Forum* and *Saturday Night* magazine. On the rise of the CCF see McNaught, *A Prophet in Politics*, S. M. Lipset, *Agrarian Socialism* (Berkeley: University of California Press, 1959), Dean McHenry, *The Third Force in Canada: the Co-operative Commonwealth Federation, 1932-1948* (Berkeley: University of California Press, 1950), and Leo Zakuta, *A Protest Movement Becalmed* (Toronto: University of Toronto Press, 1964). There is a good section on this period in the centennial anthology edited by Morris Careless and Craig Brown, *The Canadians 1867-1967* (Toronto: Macmillan, 1967). A colourful account of life in the relief camps and of the Ottawa trek is Ronald Liversedge's *Recollections of the On-To-Ottawa Trek, 1935* (Vancouver, privately printed, n.d.).

For Chapter V, in addition to the books by McNaught, Lipset, and Zakuta already mentioned, the collected essays of Frank Underhill—one of the founding members of the League for Social Reconstruction and the principal draftsman of the Regina Manifesto—*In Search of Canadian Liberalism* (Toronto: Macmillan, 1960), are particularly useful. The development of the CCF is covered in detail in the present author's

The Anatomy of a Party: The National CCF, 1933-1961 (Toronto: University of Toronto Press, 1969).

Recommended for Chapter VI are Gad Horowitz, *Canadian Labour in Politics* (Toronto: University of Toronto Press, 1968), Dale Thomson's *Louis St. Laurent, Canadian* (Toronto: Macmillan, 1967), and J. L. Granatstein, *The Politics of Survival: The Conservative Party of Canada, 1939-1945* (Toronto: University of Toronto Press, 1967). In addition, J. W. Pickersgill's edition of Mackenzie King's diaries, *The Mackenzie King Record*, vol. I: *1939-44* (Toronto: University of Toronto Press, 1960) should be consulted for references to the CCF.

The two obvious sources for Chapter VII are C. B. Macpherson's *Democracy in Alberta* (Toronto: University of Toronto Press, 1953), which provides the best discussion of the nature and background of social credit theory, and John Irving's *The Social Credit Movement in Alberta* (Toronto: University of Toronto Press, 1959). Irving's book examines closely the rise of Aberhart and the response of the people. Read in conjunction with Macpherson, the student will gain a thorough and broad picture of the movement. An interesting examination and defense of Macpherson's argument is found in the issues of *Canadian Forum* for November, December and January, 1954-55. S. M. Lipset's two part review of the book and Macpherson's reply show two interesting approaches to the analysis of the Canadian party system.

On the later history of Social Credit the only source is Macpherson's volume, which carries the story up to 1949. For British Columbia, Margaret Ormsby's *British Columbia: A History* (Toronto: Macmillan, 1958) is useful, but it should be supplemented for this period by *Bennett*, (Toronto: McClelland and Stewart, 1966), a biography of the Premier by Paddy Sherman.

Index

A

Aberhart, William: xii; as parliamentarian, 39; introduces Social Credit, 81; background, 83; religious activities, 84; authoritarian nature, 84-5; contacts with Douglas, 86, 95; on implementing Social Credit in Alberta, 87; Social Credit campaign, 88; and Social Credit crusade, 90; no plans for national party, 92; compared to Woodsworth, 93, 111; death, 98; legacy, 102

Angus, Henry: 89

B

Bennett, R. B.: response to depression, 47; attitude to trekkers, 48-9

Bennett, W. A. C.: Premier of British Columbia, 99-101, 102-3; attitudes toward legislature, 39, 100; as separatist, 102, 103

British Columbia: economic conditions, 5; politics, 100-3

Brownlee, John; Premier of Alberta, 80, 87, 89

C

Caouette, Réal: 92

Cameron, Colin: 77

Canadian Congress of Labour: endorses CCF, 74; unites with TLC, 77

Canadian Labour Congress: formation, 77; co-operates with CCF to form new party, 77

Coldwell, M. J.: as parliamentarian, 39; leader of Saskatchewan ILP, 51; and Woodsworth, 53; dedication to party, 61; becomes leader of CCF, 69; defeated in 1958, 77

Conservative party: 108

Co-operative commonwealth: defined, 51

Co-operative Commonwealth Federation: xi, 6; attitudes of MPs, 39; formation, 55; goals and program, 57, 58-9; public reaction to, 60-1, 74; character as movement, 61; varieties of socialism in, 61-2; 1935 election, 62-3; in House of Commons, 63-4; provincial sections, 65; and war, 65-6; growing influence, 69-71; success in Ontario and Saskatchewan, 72; source of funds, 75; and trade union movement, 74-5; revision of policy, 75-6; Winnipeg Declaration, 76; co-operates with CLC to form new party, 77; attitudes towards new party idea, 77; assessment of, 78-9; in British Columbia, 101

Crerar, T. A.: and Progressives, 26, 29, 30-4

D

Depression: 40-56; and wages, 42; and impact on prairies, 43-6; end of, 67

Diefenbaker, John: 76

Douglas, Major C. H.: founder of Social Credit, 81; visits Alberta, 86; before Canadian House of Commons, 92; offers advice to Aberhart, 95

Douglas, T. C.: forms political group in Weyburn, 52; in House of Commons, 63; as Premier of Saskatchewan, 75; becomes leader of NDP, 77

F

"Farmers' Platform": 23, 26

Forke, Robert: 34

G

Gardiner, Robert: 51
Gillis, Clarence: 66, 67
"Ginger Group": 35; and "Labour Group," 37
Grain market: 2; price of wheat, 27; Wheat Board, 29-30

I

Independent Labour Party: 51, 52
Irvine, William: 7, 8; and Non-Partisan League, 24; *The Farmers in Politics*, 24; and Woodsworth as Labour group, 37; and Social Credit, 81
Irving, John: xii, 91, 93

K

Keynes, J. M.: 67
King, W. L. M.: and the west, 30, 31; and Progressives, 31-6; back in office, 63; tribute to Woodsworth, 66; fear of CCF, 70, 78; moves party to left, 106
Knowles, Stanley: as parliamentarian, 39, 75; defeated in 1958, 77

L

"Labour Group": 37
Leadership: importance of, 110, 111
League For Social Reconstruction: formation, 53; and Regina Manifesto, 58
Liberal party: 108
Lipset, S. M.: iv, 55, 70
Liversedge, Ron: 48
Low, Solon: 98

M

McGeer, Gerry: 89
MacInnis, Grace: 64
McNaught, K.: 21
Macphail, Agnes: 53
Macpherson, C. B.: xii, 83, 98
Manning, Ernest C.: Aberhart's assistant, 85; campaigning for Social Credit, 88; succeeds Aberhart, 91; as Premier, 98; publishes book, 99; at Federal-Provincial Conference, 1967, 103
Masters, D. C.: 21

Meighen, Arthur: and farmers, 30; and Progressives, 32; and constitutional crisis, 36; defeated by Noseworthy, 71; attitude to CCF, 74
Morton, W. L.: 25; 33

N

National Progressive Party: founded, 26; *see also* Progressives
New Democratic Party; formation, 77; ideology, 104
Nicholson, A. M.: 46
Non-Partisan League: 23, 24
Noseworthy, Joseph: defeats Meighen, 71

O

One Big Union: formation, 15, 16; and RCMP, 16; leaders, 16; and Winnipeg strike, 22
Ottawa trek: 47-8

P

Porter, John: 108
Progressives: 29-39; division between Alberta and Manitoba wings, 29, 31-3; elected in 1921, 31; in House of Commons, 33-9; Ginger Group, 35-6; decline, 36; legacy, 37-8; *see also* National Progressive Party

R

Regina Manifesto: 58-9
Rowell-Sirois Commission: 43

S

Scott, Frank: 52
Social Credit: x, xii; and MPs, 39; origins, 80; economic and political theory, 81-3; movement becomes a party, 87; enthusiasm for, 88, 89; and farmers, 95; compared to CCF, 94; in office, 95, 96, 97; national party, 98-9; in British Columbia, 98-101; British Columbia and Alberta versions, 101; as conservative force, 101
Socialism: attitudes toward, 54
Socialist parties: 10, 11, 15
Stevens, H. H.: and Reconstruction party, 62
St. Laurent, Louis: view of CCF, 106

T

Thatcher, Ross: 103
Thompson, Robert: 99
Trades and Labour Congress: 77

U

Underhill, Frank: 52; and Regina Manifesto, 58
Unions: formation, 12; growth, 14; social acceptance, 108
Union Nationale party: 107
United Farmers of Alberta: iii; and invitation to conference, 51; and CCF, 80; government of Alberta, 80; influence on Alberta politics, 90
United Farmers of Manitoba: xii; and Independent Labour Party, 52
United Farmers of Ontario: xi

W

Western Canada: politics of, compared with other provinces, 109-110
Western Labour Political Parties: first conference, 50; 1932 conference, 53

Wheat Farmer: and geography and climate, 2; and grain market, 2-3; insecurity of, 1-4; and National Policy, 3; Grain Growers' Associations, 9; compared with other farmers, 109-10
Williams, George: 52; and Woodsworth, 53
Winnipeg general strike: xiii; 17-22; and OBU, 17; opposition to, 18, 19; reaction to, 18; sympathetic strikes, 18; Robson Report on, 21; farmers' reaction, 22-3
Wood, Henry Wise: 13; philosophy, 25, 26; and Progressives, 29ff; retirement, 51; birthplace, 110
Woodsworth, J. S.: and social gospel, 7, 8; and Non-Partisan League, 24; and Progressives, 35; and Labour group, 36; and depression, 40; and 1932 conference of Western Labour Political Parties, 53; and LSR, 53; and formation of Commonwealth Party, 53; character, 53-4; chosen CCF leader, 59; opposition to war, 65-6; retirement and death, 69; compared with Aberhart, 111
Workers: insecurity, 4